THE CANNABIS CONUNDRUM

While Others Blow Smoke, These Experts Start to Clear the Air

Dr. Rob Streisfeld

"Together with other industry experts, insiders, and influencers"

TABLE OF CONTENTS

CHAPTER 10

CAN CANNABIS BE SUSTAINABLE?

The Cannabis Conundrum

PREFACE

"We are now faced with the fact that tomorrow is today. We are confronted with the fierce urgency of now. In this unfolding conundrum of life and history, there "is" such a thing as being too late." - Martin Luther King, Jr.

While the above is neither Dr. King's most popular quote, or even meant to address the same social issue for that matter, his words hold an undeniable relevance to the current state surrounding Cannabis in modern society.

A conundrum represents, by definition, an intricate and difficult problem. In this case, the numerous and varied factors to consider when the topic of cannabis takes center stage. Here, a nearly century-old chess game driven by capitalists and misinformation, link together politics, healthcare, banking and finance, law, social justice and cultural evolution ...over a plant. Considered a simple weed by many, but having over 500 different compounds identified, which offer important nutritional, medical and industrial applications, in no way is this amazing gift of Nature "simple". With a rapidly increasing scientific understanding, combined with a growing global acceptance, we are now faced with the fact that what many thought was a long way off tomorrow, is actually upon us today.

And who are the pawns in this chess game; the ones who are moved around and surrendered by those in control? The unfortunate answer is the gross majority. Myself, you, your children, your neighbors, and even your pets. The planet we live on, too.

More dramatic is the impact on minorities and/or any individual or group who threatens the establishment's grip on the status quo. We are truly confronted with the fierce urgency of now.

Modern science has tried to synthesize and replicate many safe and effective natural remedies, and use patents and programmed health providers to overprescribe and overcharge the sick and needy. From infants to the elderly, they are given toxic pharmaceuticals with a myriad of side effects, when good diet, plant-based medicines, and love are all they really need. Cannabis, once considered a dangerous "gate way" drug, is now being used to help treat addictions of alcohol, opioid-based medications, and other harmful substances while also supporting those suffering from PTSD (post-traumatic stress disorder), anxiety, and many other diseases.

For thousands of years, Cannabis was a valued and appreciated herb/plant commonly found in medicines and traditional remedies, incorporated into religious ceremonies, and used to make paper, rope, textiles, and more. As recent as 1941, Cannabis Sativa was listed in the U.S. Pharmacopeia and recommended by physicians. Cannabis is a true gift of Nature, far from the demonized plant that a biased media, corporate greed, and an underlying racist agenda makes it out to be.

However, times are once again changing. We are now seeing a collective awakening to the power of plants, led by a long-standing history and a multitude of uses that Cannabis offers. We have politicians from both sides seeing the potential of the plant. There are currently 30 states with some type of law permitting Cannabis use, either for medical or adult-use or both with bills submitted on the Federal level. We have the global medical community excited about the role that Cannabis and its compounds can play in treating disease while improving health and well-being. Many are anticipating the legalization of Industrial Hemp with the passage of the 2018 Farm Bill. Although still a young and budding industry, states where Cannabis has been legalized are seeing a reduction, not increase, in teen use, DUI fatalities, and drug overdoses. Let's not forget the large revenue the states are seeing from taxes, tourism and more. There are still issues such as banking, lab testing and quality control, proper dosing, etc., that need to be sorted out, many, if not all, are addressed in the chapters of this book.

The time for Cannabis is now! While progress has been made, there is still a long way to go. As MLK Jr stated above, there "is" such a thing as too late.

There's still a lot of confusion and a definite need for quality education on the subject. With that in mind, I've identified some key thought leaders in the Cannabis movement who collectively share some insight... to help clear the air and guide us through "The Cannabis Conundrum" we are currently in the midst of.

From researchers to physicians, established CEOs to young entrepreneurs, marketing mavens to mom's trying to find answers for their sick child, from farmers to our veterans who deserve the best options we can provide, this book is for you. For us to be successful, we need to do this together... as a community, a society, and an industry.

Shout Outs! (*aka* Acknowledgements)

"Feeling gratitude and not expressing it is like wrapping a present and not giving it." —William Arthur Ward

I want to take this time to express my sincere gratitude to everyone who contributed towards the creation and success of this book. A big "Thank You" to the contributing authors, editors, marketers, consumers, critics, my fans and followers. I also want to thank all those in the Industry who operate ethically and with integrity, advocating for both the plant and the planet.

This book would not have been possible without my friends and family, those who not only celebrate the "highs" but who also show up with love and support when times get low. I am lucky to have so many amazing people in my life. It is truly inspiring when spending time with you all, especially those with kids. We must all work hard to protect the future of the next generation.

A special mention goes out to:
My partners and colleagues at BeyondBrands
The team at CannabisRadio.com
Rakesh M, for helping me stay grounded while keeping my eyes on the stars
Walter J, my friend and partner on this project
Mark, my amazing Dad
Kevin, my younger "big" brother and family, especially J & T.
Lori, my life partner and best friend. Grateful to share this journey with you and your kids, S & J.

Finally, I wouldn't be the person I am without the love and support of family members who are no longer with us in physical form… their memories live on and their impact will never be forgotten.

Chapter 1

Vis Medicatrix Naturae - The Healing Power of Nature

Rob "Doc Rob" Streisfeld, NMD

While the excitement of the emerging industry is palpable, for many years there has been controversies, debates and countless conundrums surrounding Cannabis. The history of this plant is tainted with misinformation campaigns and racial undertones. We were told for decades that it is a gateway drug, dangerous and highly addictive, and that it possesses no known medical benefit. We now know that there are numerous health benefits, that it appears to be far safer and less addictive than alcohol, and it is now even being used to help people get off harmful opioid-based drugs, many of which have been legal and wreaking havoc in our communities at unprecedented levels.

Even something as basic as what to call it, i.e.: Cannabis, Hemp, Marijuana, Pot, Ganja, Weed, Grass, Herb, Bud, Mary Jane, etc., or comparing and choosing different ways to consume it, i.e.: smoking, eating, vaping, ingesting orally, applying topically, or even insertion rectally, can make your head spin. The modern cannabis industry is taking shape with legalization slowly spreading nationally and across the globe. With an exponential growth not seen since the tech boom of the 1980s, it is becoming more and more likely that cannabis will have an impact on your life, personally, professionally, or both.

How do you feel or react to a friend or family member who may be dealing with an illness, and expresses interest in trying medical marijuana as a treatment option? What if you or a loved one becomes a patient and wants to go on vacation or business trip, will you be able to take your cannabis medication with you? Will you educate your children about the safe and responsible use of cannabis, similar to conversations about alcohol and safe sex? Maybe you own a company in a state that has legalized cannabis for medical or adult use, and you are now forced to reevaluate your HR policies, your approach to drug testing and the impact on employee health insurance coverage. A legal industrial hemp industry looks to disrupt many long standing and inefficient industries, those currently leaving large carbon footprints and destroying our planet. While working to reduce the amount of petroleum-based plastics, chemicals, pesticides, and other man-made compounds negatively impacting our environment, we will see cannabis derivatives integrated or replacing everyday items from clothing to car parts, building materials to bio-fuels. Where Cannabis has been legalized, the industry has already had a noticeable effect on housing, employment, tax revenue and much more. The positive impact has far outweighed the negative, but there's no denying growing pains still exist.

As the walls of prohibition start to crumble around the world, it is both imperative and feasible to get a better understanding of cannabis, whether you personally use it or not. The scientific community is working to clarify misconceptions. The political landscape is shifting towards greater acceptance. Market research suggests that Cannabis will have nearly a $150 billion-dollar market value by 2025. With big money on the table, the risk of history repeating itself looms and it becomes imperative to become more acquainted with the subject.

Recognizing that my relationship and experiences with this plant are surely different from yours, and nearly everyone else's for that matter, we encounter our first conundrum. Good experiences or bad, long time user or exploring for the first time, we all have our own viewpoint. Your perception and acceptance of Cannabis may be skewed by where and when you grew up, your environment and education level, or personal experience such as whether or not you "experimented" in college.

Fortunate for me, I grew up in the beautiful Catskill Mountains of New York, a few miles from the historic Woodstock Festival of '69. My perception of a plant called Marijuana resonated with things like peace and love, great music, and community more than with anything negative or harmful. I had the opportunity to grow up interacting with Nature. I climbed trees, went swimming and fished in the lakes, played Little League and loved skiing in the winter. Like many, we had a vegetable garden in the Spring/Summer and Grandma's cherry tomatoes were always something to look forward to. We shopped locally as much as possible and I remember going to the farmer's market, excited to see all the different things they had. I believe this connection with Nature planted the seed which helped shape the life and career I have now.

While my childhood experiences provided stable roots, my education and career focus has allowed me to branch out and truly appreciate Cannabis, as well as many other gifts from Nature. As someone who has studied a great deal about this amazing but complicated plant, and with respect to Mother Nature, this book was assembled so that in addition to my own experiences, I can invite others to share their experiences and perspectives as part of an evolving conversation.

3

In all honesty, I struggled a bit on the scope of content I wanted to contribute in this book. There are so many aspects of this subject requiring discussion and debate, including but not limited to its role in healthcare, legal matters, banking and financial implications, and perhaps even how many times you should use puns in a chapter of a book. Hehe

I finally came to realize that the best thing to do is share from my own journey and experiences. You may not be familiar with who I am, or why I find it so important to contribute to the conversation, so the following is meant to provide a little context to my personal perspective and considerations, both positive and negative, while addressing some of the key aspects of Cannabis. Based on my experience and education, I feel qualified to share, and hope you agree.

B.S. in Human Biology

It all started in college. Yes, I am one of those who experimented with Cannabis while away at school. I found it helped with my pain, sleep, stress management and even improved my ability to focus. My studies in school were revolved around Biology and Anthropology. My interests had always been to work in the healthcare industry, but after volunteering in a local area hospital pharmacy, I quickly became disenfranchised with the plethora of pills being pushed on the patients. (Say that five times fast.) Learning about traditional cultures, their diets and rituals, a common theme presented. They all had a profound respect for Nature. Very often their lives depended on it. They also relied on a strong community and a commitment to survival using whatever Nature provided. The practical use of herbs in healing, in the diet, and for spiritual practice can be found in societies dating back thousands of years.

4

This most definitely included the use of Cannabis.

Naturopathic Doctor

My experience as a Doctor of Naturopathic Medicine has helped provide insight on how the various cannabis compounds and delivery systems may affect the body. When using Cannabis to address a health condition or to promote overall well-being, it is important to properly dose and consider any interactions with other medications, supplements, or herbs. Though the overall safety is impressive, even with children, it is still recommended to work with a health professional, especially when looking to integrate Cannabis into a treatment protocol for a complex or chronic disease. Naturopathic Doctors believe in the healing power of Nature (Vis Medicatrix Naturae), as well as the body's own ability to heal itself. We also look to identify the underlying cause of disease and treat the whole person (Tolle Causam).

My career path has been intentionally less focused on individual patient care and more so directed towards health education and innovation. *Docere,* or "Doctor as Teacher" is another key principle of being a Naturopathic Physician. With an obvious comfort when on stage or in front of an audience, and a tendency to be naturally loquacious, it has become one of the principles I hold most dear. As a professor, podcast host, and spokesperson for industry leading brands in the Natural Products & Foods Industry, I've had the opportunity and privilege to educate, engage, and entertain on a variety of subjects. I've enjoyed a "behind the scenes" look working with some amazing companies, witnessing the ups and downs, benefits and challenges, and inevitable growing pains an emerging and disruptive industry goes through. Most people had never heard of probiotics or thought to try an acai bowl with chia seeds a few years ago, but that's no longer the case today. With increased education, scientific research, and improving quality control in cultivation and manufacturing, Cannabis compounds and derivatives will too find their place in doctor's offices, pharmacies, supermarkets, restaurants and health food stores. If they haven't already, there's a good chance they will soon end up in your own home as well.

I've seen first-hand the way cannabis relieves pain, assists digestion and GI function, helps with sleep, and supports an individual's Endocannabinoid system, improving overall well-being.

Cannabis can effectively treat disease, both acute and chronic, and at the same time will play a role in disease prevention, helping optimize a person's health and vitality. Lifestyle and dietary changes also need to be considered. At least when you exercise, you will soon be able to use a form of Cannabis to assist with inflammation, pain, and aid in recovery too.

An article I once wrote referred to Cannabis as a "gateway" herb. My hope is that as result of the attention this one plant is getting, for all its proven health benefits, a door to greater acceptance of herbal medicine and plant-based healing will open. It is important to recognize, in the effort to both prevent and treat disease, that there are many safe and effective natural remedies and plant based/herbal options available. From Asia to the Amazon, many of these have been used for centuries, having proven efficacy and scientific standards. In fact, organizations such as the American Herbal Products Association (AHPA) help promote quality standards and serve as a voice for herbal products and consumer safety. AHPA's

Cannabis committee, which I am proud member of, is just one example of the many organizations working to further legitimize Cannabis as a safe, herbal option. Be assured, there's a global community of scientists, researchers, medical professionals and industry experts who are focused on identifying the pros and cons of Cannabis. I'm honored and proud to play an active role in reintroducing this plant back to the world.

Natural Foods Chef

As a trained chef, I consider Cannabis more as an herb or vegetable, a plant-based superfood in fact, similar to kale, almonds, and cacao. Herbs like Rosemary and Sage, while today commonly used in cooking to infuse flavor, were traditionally valued for the ability to impart a physical effect to the person consuming it, or to the food itself. We drink herbal teas like Chamomile, Valerian root and Lavender to reduce anxiety and aid sleep. We know that chocolate contains magnesium and our body often craves it when deficient. There is an art to cooking, and in addition to the esthetic appeal, I am truly impressed when ingredient choices are made with nutritional considerations, offering both flavor and functionality.

I hope you can appreciate that a chef is an artist, carefully blending a palate of ingredients to create smells and flavors, intending to stimulate an experience of some kind. Some are best served raw, others require a cooking method of some type. The properties, including nutritional benefits, often change as we manipulate something from its Nature-given form. This transformation can be positive, as seen when making nutrients more bioavailable through fermentation, but can also prove negative like when heating certain oils at too high a temperature.

We are continually exploring more ways to use Cannabis as a food, infusing extracts into snacks, beverages, and entrees. Many are familiar with popular edibles in the form of brownies, cookies, gummies, and chocolates. The emerging industry now offers a much wider assortment of consumables, products ranging from sparkling herbal tonics to infused ice cream and pizza. A true spectrum of options tantalizes the taste buds, from gourmet cuisine to traditional comfort food. We also see the potential for fresh leaves in salads, blending Cannabis/Hemp in to smoothies, juicing it like wheatgrass shots, and more. Did you know that when you eat Cannabis raw, even though there is a form of THC in it (THC-A), you can't and won't get "high"?

The US already imports a significant amount of hemp protein powders, hemp seed oils, and hemp fiber for use in food and supplements. Though there remains some confusion as to what parts of the plant are being used and the difference between Marijuana and Hemp, the nutritional benefits are well established. With its ability to grow in a variety of climates and conditions, hemp is a much-needed option for the future of our food supply. As stated earlier, Cannabis/Hemp products have been used for thousands of years in cultures all over the globe. With the passage of the 2018 Farm Bill, the dream of many to see hemp legal and growing throughout the United States again will soon become realized.

While my undergraduate studies focused on traditional diets, cultures, and natural remedies, my culinary school training took that knowledge to the next level, helping me see the potential of using food as medicine first hand. I find it amazing and inspiring to watch the culinary community work to infuse Cannabis into food products, exploring how this plant and others can be better incorporated into our daily lifestyles.

Please keep in mind, that whether consuming socially, medically, or for nutritional purposes, it is important to always consume responsibly.

Consultant for Dietary Supplements and Natural, Functional Foods

With this increasing interest in the plant around the world, there are numerous clinical studies and research efforts working towards a better understanding of Cannabis and the over 500 compounds found within. With both excitement and trepidation, I anticipate some big developments and challenges as demand continues to grow. Will the CBD market become saturated? How will technology and innovation impact the quality and price of Cannabis products? How do you determine what strain or cannabis product is best for you? Which brands will survive and thrive in this rapidly changing market?

I've already mentioned a bit of my over fifteen years of experience working with dietary supplements and natural, healthy foods. There is great potential for cannabis-based products to be used effectively as dietary supplements, infused in food & beverages, cosmeceuticals, and more. Science has already begun to confirm that the whole plant, as Nature designed it, seems to work better than when isolating individual components. That doesn't mean there aren't scenarios where an individual need to use or incorporate an isolated compound. We also see that some people benefit from lower doses while others require higher potencies, yet the full understanding of why is still yet to be determined. Some people prefer to abstain from products that produce a euphoric, psychoactive effect or "high", while others such as those facing terminal illness, welcome the levity and find comfort in the experience.

Conscious Consumer Advocate

Whether you are aware of it or not, anything you put in or on your body is a choice you make. It is your responsibility to do research, become more educated, and to find what works best for you. There are, and always will be, those individuals and companies who are just looking to make money on the current trends, taking advantage of desperate or uninformed people. While this is inevitable, there are also many people with real health issues who rely on this plant and need consistent access to safe, quality products and qualified health practitioners to support and advise them. Fortunately, an increasing number of health professionals and conscious consumers alike are becoming more educated, helping to hold cannabis growers and manufacturers to a high standard. Testing of materials, ingredients and finished products are important. Thankfully, Good Manufacturing Practices (GMPs) and other standards have already been established by the dietary supplement and food industries and are being utilized by Cannabis companies more each day.

There's a huge industry exploding on the scene, creating jobs, revenue, consumer products, and more. We see a wide range of professionals from various industries, applying their skills and getting involved in the Cannabis Industry. Big Alcohol has entered the game along with Big Tobacco and Big Pharma. The end to prohibition no longer seems unattainable and the "Green Rush", as it is often referred to, is upon us.

By sharing the content above, I hope that I have provided

some insight and spurred your interest to continue forward. Addressing Cannabis and its reintroduction into modern society, as this book attempts to do, is a conundrum in itself. It is likely that in doing so, we actually raise more questions than we are able to provide concrete answers. The chapters which follow are written by a select group of contributors, intended to help cover a wide range of content. It should soon become obvious that there are numerous perspectives and nuances to consider, and that while this chapter has come to an end, this is just the beginning of the conversation.

Chapter 2

Canna-Biz Goes Legit: Marijuana's Long, Tough Climb into the Light of the Modern Business World

Denise A. Pollicella, Esq.

Cannabis aka Marijuana has always been a business. Since before the 1937 Tax Act, it was a commonly used medicine. But it took the Controlled Substances Act of 1971 to make it big business. Prohibition simply made it a less available, more expensive drug, as well as a number one seller for dangerous cartels. It may not have been taxed or tested, but it has never stopped being a commodity, and it has never stopped being a business.

Unfortunately, it has taken us in the United States much longer to come to our senses about the silliness and futility of marijuana prohibition than it did for alcohol. The world into which medical cannabis, industrial hemp and recreational marijuana are emerging is more interconnected, complex and rule-intensive. Now, we must try to extract it out of a web of hundreds of laws, formed over decades and designed to keep marijuana out of every facet of our lives, the ever-present shadow of its illegal federal status casting doubt on every step into the light.

So, how do we transition cannabis from back alley to main street? It is all well and good that we have begun to legally protect the use and cultivation of marijuana in most states, but without legal federal status, and without the infrastructure that exists to support all other businesses, how can we protect its manufacture and distribution? How, indeed, does one go from tie-dyed to suit and tie?

The Federal Problem

The most obvious and direct challenge to operating a cannabis business is its federally illegal status. If you live in one of the nearly thirty states that have decriminalized marijuana for medical purposes or legalized it for recreational adult use, it can be easy to forget that we still have not de-scheduled it. According to the United States Government, it is still, today, one of the most dangerous drugs on the planet. That distinction means that it is illegal in the federal 'space,' so marijuana cannot be sold on the internet, for example, or shipped through the US Postal Service. One cannot patent a particularly awesome sativa genetic or register a marijuana use trademark through the US Patent and Trademark Office. You cannot trade it on the New York Stock Exchange, use it as collateral for a Small Business Administration loan, drive it across state lines, or put it in an FDIC insured bank. Pharmacies cannot dispense it and doctors cannot prescribe it. Of course, you still have to pay taxes on your "ill-gotten gains" from the sale of marijuana to the IRS.

In addition to being unable to legally operate in the federal realm, there remains the threat of prosecution under federal law. You do not need to visit conspiracy theories to understand the very real profit motive behind these prosecutions, which support civil asset-forfeiture and related statutes like the Racketeer Influenced and Corrupt Organizations Act (RICO), which award attorney fees and treble damages. This alone is disincentive enough to keep the banking, lending, real estate and insurance industries away from marijuana businesses.

Dubious legal status on the Federal level, no banking, lending, and high taxes. Add in the ignorance and social stigma of the War on Drugs which still hangs in the air. Just the kind of business incubator every budding entrepreneur dream of. Great! Let's also add some regulations.

The State Regulatory Barriers

You have to hand it to the states for their initiative, or more ac-curately, their initiatives. Impatient with the political gridlock plaguing our legislatures, voters have taken to the polls in an effort to force cannabis into legal status. Unfortunately, whether it was through ballot initiative or legislation, this plant has rapidly gone from so illegal we didn't need any rules, to so highly regulated it is almost not worth the bother.

This rule-making on an epic scale across the country comes from a combination of fear of political reprisals, residual drug war ignorance, concern over liability exposure, an effort to draft pathways around federal law, and self-dealing designed to enrich the privileged. Basically, just a bunch of ignorance and fear.

As it stands, some modicum of state regulation is needed to protect residents in marijuana states. It also tends to send a message to the US Attorney's office that it will not be operat-ing on friendly turf if it pursues prosecutions. From a business perspective, however, the states have created unnecessary bureaucracies. Exploring the motives and rationale behind this regulatory hell may help those starting out in this business to understand what lies ahead.

First, cannabis has not been a commercial good for over fifty years, so we quite literally had a blank slate to work from. Unfortunately, we started off badly, regulating it like it is dangerous, when the most dangerous thing about marijuana is and was its illegal status. Ignorance of marijuana's relative safety is nothing more than laziness and an unwillingness to admit that marijuana prohibition is another in a long line of mistakes our young nation has made. That fear of the unknown, that Pavlovian reaction to the word "marijuana", translated into meaningless overregulation.

Next, politicians seeking to protect their seats in socially conservative districts have been besieged by anti-marijuana groups increasingly desperate in the face of certain defeat. This nod to fear and ignorance resulted in unnecessary and nonsensical rule-making based on bias instead of fact.

Then there are municipal officials. These local civil servants are truly on the front lines, fielding hundreds of phone calls, petitions, angry constituents and impatient developers. While some local ordinance language is a symptom of the struggle municipal attorneys are having trying to protect their clients in the course of authorizing federally illegal conduct, the unnecessary, repetitive crap finding its way into municipal codes is bad for everybody. Passing onerous state administrative rules into a city's ordinance is anathema to economic development and an administrative burden on staff that will have to be constantly revised with developing state law. Massive state regulatory structures are already in place across the nation to en sure that these licensed businesses behave. Other than zoning, local ordinances could, and should, consist of a one-sentence reference to state law and be done with it.

Last, but always making sure they are never least, are the inside traders. Riding the fence just this side of campaign finance law lies the partnership between rich white guys and the law-makers trying to be rich white guys. Successful business people do not like competition, so they lobby lawmakers to legislate state-level monopolies. This competition-free environment stifles innovation, keeps quality low, artificially inflates prices and denies most middle-income people entrée into this market.

The reality is that a still uninhabitable federal climate combined with burdensome state regulations make it nearly impossible for anyone but millionaires to become pot barons, and have put owning a cannabis company out of reach for most of us. That is where complex structuring, lopsided partnerships, crowd-funded investing, private lending and dubious banking alternatives have all made an entrance. These types of practices are risky for all businesses. Adding a federally illegal controlled substance and removing safety nets like FDIC insured deposits and bankruptcy protections makes canna-business that much riskier.

Who's In, Who's Out, and How Creative is Too Creative

Think about the basics of what every new business needs to get off the ground today: a name, a bank account, some capital, advertising, supplies, insurance, a building and perhaps a loan. Now take away the bank and the lending. If you want to start a business but you cannot get an SBA loan, cannot use your home equity line of credit, and cannot use your grow equipment, product or business as collateral, then you must be entirely self-funded out of liquid personal assets. This reality has created three main routes into the industry: millionaires; pooled capital through unstructured investment groups and joint ventures; and those without enough capital but want to give it a go anyway. Regardless of the route by which one enters, the hazards are the same. The key is in recognizing and mitigating risk. But why bother worrying about risk when everything you do is federally illegal anyway?

The threat of more civilized RICO prosecutions seems less scary than the aggressive drug task force raids of the past, and where entrepreneurial spirit pushes the boundaries of criminal conduct, you will always find those willing to step over to gain an advantage. Add to that marijuana's new quasi-legal status and broader social acceptance, and there is an increasing sense that everybody's doing it, so why can't I.

In fact, most legal hazards are a common threat to all businesses and are not specific to the cannabis industry. Any good transactional attorney counsels her clients on risk management strategies that allow them to thrive and grow without running afoul of tax law and the standard plethora of white collar crimes.

For those operating in the nascent cannabis industry, some rule-breaking just goes with the territory: possession, manufacturing and distribution of a controlled substance, money laundering, conspiracy and wire fraud. Even to the extent of operating a drug house. The only thing separating most of us from federal prison is some rare good sense on the part of the feds. Even assuming this really awkward truce holds though, there are still pitfalls which are not as apparent, but are equally treacherous and difficult to avoid.

One example is the banking problem. Banks are federally insured financial deposit and lending institutions, and absent a blanket federal immunity guarantee for taking drug money, most banks have declined. However, the pressure to use a bank account is intense, and it is wildly inconvenient to do business without one. You cannot write checks or use a business credit card, wire funds, order supplies online, or lend money, or invest. Keeping massive amounts of cash is unsafe, not only because it is uninsured if it is lost, stolen or destroyed, but because failing to deposit money in a bank can be prima facie evidence of tax evasion. Desperate, you lie, telling the assistant bank manager you opened an herbal tea store. Viola, Bank fraud! You make multiple small cash deposits in different banks to avoid attention, also a crime. You open an account for a shell company and use that for your deposits. Still a crime.

Real estate is another hurdle. It is really hard to find a property owner willing to lease to a cannabis tenant. There is little one can do to assuage a prospective landlord's fear that he could be charged for operating a drug house and his property seized. You cannot honestly represent that the risk is zero, and a lease agreement then either comes off the table, or the rent becomes so expensive you might as well buy.

Insurance is yet another problem. In addition to being nearly cost-prohibitive, it is difficult to find and there is a temptation to be coy about your business. Don't. Carrying insurance on a gardening supply warehouse will not do you any good when your claim agent visits and finds a grow facility. You will be

19

denied coverage and probably charged with insurance fraud. Title insurance companies willing to handle a real estate transaction for this industry have become like unicorns. We hear they exist, but nobody can find one.

Financing is at the root of the most creative business planning. If you are not wealthy, and you cannot get a loan, and you cannot refinance your house, alternative funding becomes your only option. You do online crowd-funding, or take personal unsecured loans from friends and family, and now your silent partners are in your drug cartel, and on it goes.

Offshore banks, precious metal conversion, hiding assets to avoid taxation. Creative strategies with ambiguous legal standing have always been a part of capitalism, but marihuana businesses will be in a fishbowl for the foreseeable future, and those still unfriendly to the cannabis industry will not hesitate to seek out ways to take down the reckless.

With the road ahead plagued by legal, regulatory and societal road blocks, one must go into this industry business-savvy, well-funded, and thoroughly educated on the risk for any reasonable chance at success. Faced with such daunting challenges, it is incredible that so many are willing to try, but green-rush fever has gripped the country, fueled by the rare opportunity to get in on the ground floor of an already multi-billion-dollar market.

How to Plan for a Future in Canna-Biz

Being a pot baron sounds awfully cool. The reality is, however, that there are no short cuts. There is little counsel to give at this point to those crazy enough to brave the perils of a brand-new industry that makes and sells a Schedule I controlled substance. Even though the road forward may be uncertain, there are three basics to remember that can provide as steady a foundation as possible: 1. Never lie. It is a difficult transition for those used to hiding their activities for years, but it is a necessary one. Lying to banks, insurance companies, state regulators and the IRS all have severe and permanent consequences. 2. Be flexible, yet conservative in your planning. This industry is a roller coaster of regulation. You must be able to adapt financially and legally with the changing laws while respecting clear legal boundaries. 3. Surround yourself with qualified professionals so that you remain fully informed. Accountants and attorneys will be there to give you the counsel needed to more safely grow your business.

To you budding entrepreneurs, we will get there. Public opinion polls continue to show positive attitudes toward medical and recreational cannabis, and full legalization is on the horizon, making this choppy regulatory mess a temporary one. In the meantime, hang on and enjoy the ride.

The difference between a conundrum, which is defined as an intricate and difficult problem, and a cannabis conundrum, is that the "cannabis conundrum" is purely artificial, man-made, and self-inflicted. History has taken a vastly useful plant and made it the subject of a trumped-up controversy, which never would have happened if the plant was useless. Should we be surprised that our prohibition-era pot role models like Cheech and Chong were irresponsible wastoids? Was their popularity a symptom of the plant, or a symptom of prohibition? Was the country prejudiced against the actual plant itself, or the folks who used it to symbolize that they can think for themselves?

Kenny Morrison

Branded Products Pioneer behind Venice Cookie Company and Cannabis Quencher, and CEO of VCC Brands

Chapter 3

As the Hemp Industry Takes Flight … Buyer Beware?

Michael Leago & William Osler Abbott

While many people are seeing more hemp products hitting the market, especially those containing Cannabidiol (CBD), behind the scenes the industry is full of challenges, confusion, and some turbulence too.

First of all, there is the need to understand Cannabis, specifically the difference between Hemp and "Marijuana" products. Hemp is not the same as marijuana, but they both come from the cannabis family. It's the same plant, but hemp has an arbitrary tetrahydrocannabinol (THC) level. By U.S. standards, it is considered hemp when the THC content falls below 0.3 percent. In comparison, the plant falls under the categorization of marijuana when above 0.3 percent THC. While it may taste, look, and smell like marijuana, hemp is traditionally grown more like corn and soy. This means big outdoor fields and wide ranging industrial value placed on the hemp stalks for the inner herd and outer fiber. Today, the demand for CBD genetics is expanding the hemp industry, however, most of the CBD Hemp is being grown more similar to its close cousin, Marijuana. This very often means the plants are primarily being used to extract oil from the leaves and buds. There's a big difference between hemp grown in the greenhouse or warehouse, versus that grown outside in a field.

"People are becoming more and more educated about the difference," Mike Leago states, the co-founder of the International Hemp Exchange (iHEMPx). Leago and his partner, Bill Abbott, believe that clarity is key. It's what the industry needs amongst the tangled misunderstood mess between buyers and sellers.

With still a large portion of the population confused about the difference between hemp and marijuana, the conundrum has impacted all levels of the industry, from the field to the shelf, and all parties involved in-between.

Launched in 2016 by Leago, the International Hemp Exchange is the first online marketplace that connects both buyers and sellers in the world of hemp. iHEMPx has communicated and worked with over 90 retail cannabidiol (CBD) vendors all over the world. The company essentially acts as a supply-chain intermediary for hemp, serving as both a stable platform for industry assistance and a resource hub for commodities that create a marketplace for people to use.

A major goal for the company is to alleviate the stress on the broker side. Abbott said that over the past year, the broker side of hemp has gotten out of control. Originally and not too long ago, many people's perspective of hemp was that it was "not an attractive or sexy industry." Others just weren't interested in buying or selling hemp with limited applications in the marketplace. When cannabidiol (CBD) extracted from hemp hit the market, all of a sudden there was a dramatic rise in interest. This negative trajectory of selling hemp products frustrated many brokers from the emerging legal marijuana industry, as well as confused farmers and consumers alike. What iHEMPx intends to do is create a positive message about

25

hemp and the industry. Both Abbott and Leago said that there has been a great amount of damage to the industry through false representation.

They believe that starting out with a trustworthy platform which connects an informed buyer and qualified seller is pivotal in launching this new stage of the understanding, creating confidence for all parties involved.

What Abbott and Leago decided for their company's main mission was to "cut through all that B.S." and "give transparency" to another option in the hemp industry.

The duo stated that there is a lot of uncertainty about the market. There's a huge demand and lots of products, and both buyer and seller sides don't really know the specifics. iHEMPx was designed to give people real options and stability in the industry. It produces real information which is accurate and representative of what is out there.

"People getting into hemp and CBD need to be really careful about where they source their information and purchase their products from," said Abbott. "They need to do their research."

iHEMPx offers just about everything. It acts as a technology platform to offer services and products while simultaneously being part of the retail industry. The company sells products wholesale seeds, flower, biomass, oil, extracts, bioplastics, and even protein food products. After all, hemp is a protein-packed plant rich in omega-3s. The idea of iHEMPx was to create supply chain, from seed-to-sale, so every bit of the plant could be used.

"Many people use Amazon for CBD and hemp products," Leago said. "But with wholesale, exchanging from business to business should be simple and affordable."

While relatively young, the company has had some interesting stories and unanticipated experiences since its inception, only a few short years ago. A good focus has been placed on the U.S. market, but there's also the conversation about how the industry is expanding internationally, including whether there's a market for it, who to sell to, what to sell and the end of the growing season. Overseas, hemp has been legalized up to 1 percent THC, specifically to sell in dispensaries for remedies.

They've witnessed an exchange between Americans and Switzerland where the Swiss traveled to the United States to pick up hemp, planning to fly it back to Switzerland (from Colorado) in an effort to expand the European market. The plane that was used was a charter jet, however, the passengers accompanying it flew coach in a separate plane. The jet was not large enough to carry the load of hemp abroad, and the jet had to make a fuel stop somewhere in between. During this time, the jet dealt with border control, the Drug Enforcement Administration (DEA) and customs. Neither Abbott nor Leago stated the result of the trip and the jet incident wasn't their story, but both Abbott and Leago witnessed it taking place. This was only one of the many entertaining, but also concerning, moments in their career so far in the industry.

Another adventure was when they headed out to Prague for a cannabis fest. At the event, there was very little differentiation between the buyer and the seller. Over and over they heard the same stories as they traveled around the globe. Everyone was trying to work in the marketplace, with very few people actually knowing what was happening. It became glaringly apparent that we are at an early stage of the industry, one that still requires significant organization and proper communication in order to be considered legitimate.

Since founding the iHempx, Leago and Abbott consider the current shifts in the industry a convergence between hemp and marijuana. They intend for the industry to grow, literally, in the direction that touches all major commodities, including but not limited to oils, textiles and building products.

With all the challenges, misunderstandings and misinformation, the negative stigma and large controversy about hemp and related products seem to be decreasing as the states become more comfortable with the idea of legal cannabis. The FDA is set to make some changes around

Cannabidiol, and the Farm Bill looks to finally legalize industrial hemp in America. "We really want to just believe it can be a conduit of real business flow," Abbott said. "The industry is so much bigger, and we want it geared toward the use of ALL the hemp plant."

"Essentially, it is far more important to avoid bad business than it is to find good business. The best CBD deal you will ever do is the CBD deal you never do."

Bill Arnold - Cannoid, LLC

Chapter 4

The Accidental Cannabis Consultant: how a conventional real estate deal opened the doors to a successful cannabis business.

Erin Phillips

While I am proud to oversee Strainwise, a company whose portfolio includes 9 branded retails stores and 4 cultivation facilities based in Colorado, with more than 130,000 square feet, we did not have an entirely auspicious start. In fact, unlike most people in the cannabis business, my husband and I never set out to be pioneers in the medicinal and recreational markets. Much has changed since he first opened our first medical marijuana store in 2010.

My husband and I worked in the real estate and mortgage industries and my husband was hired to locate a building to grow cannabis by a budding entrepreneur. Things were coming along fine and were making great progress on ensuring all the steps needed to open were in place. We had located a building and setting up a strong foundation, when we hit a wall. Colorado regulations shifted and now limited licenses to anyone with a felony in their history. The client that had hired us had a drug related arrest that dated back many years. At the time, the Colorado law stated that anyone with a felony within the previous 10 years could not obtain a medical cannabis license; but had no cutoff on drug related arrests. We had a conundrum of what to do with the building. So we jumped in with both feet. Our idea was to build up the busi-

31

ness and sell it off once it was profitable.

The interest in the emerging cannabis industry was growing, however, initial offers came mainly from nefarious types, including an offer by a large drug cartel and some other slightly less illicit interested parties, but the thought of doing business with shady buyers had us turning down numerous offers. To make matters worse, the entrepreneurial business types we thought would jump at the opportunity were nowhere to be found.

It seemed a waste to simply walk away from a building that we had helped clear hurdles, that was operating with a healthy clientele. Although we had no experience in the cannabis industry at that time, we were learning along the way and with the legalized industry being so new, in short order, we became "experts" through immersion. My husband focused on the building and infrastructure and I handled all of the necessary permitting, paperwork, licensing, retail, marketing, etc.

With a building specifically setup to legally sell medically licensed cannabis, we decided the best financial play was to see it through and become the owner/operators. The first facility opened in 2010 and we added 8 more retails stores. We were fortunate enough to be based in Colorado, the first US State to legalize recreational cannabis. Our experience throughout the process made consulting a natural progression. Not only was it financially rewarding to help others navigate the numerous hurdles and pitfalls of retail and growing operations, but it was also gratifying to be able to help others with challenges we had to learn the hard way.

When it came to the brand, personally, I wanted Strainwise to present a professional image from day one. Being parents, we didn't want the standard "pot leaves" or "green crosses" on the retail signs. We wanted our brand to convey professionalism and quality from day one. Stores with cannabis or marijuana in the name, or those stores with images of the plant draw the wrong attention and scrutiny. The last thing we wanted was groups like Mothers Against Drunk Driving or Smart Colorado putting a bull's eye on us because we had cannabis in the name or an obvious logo.

Like it or not, there is a perception that consumers of cannabis have a "stoner mentality". Statistics show that the hottest growth market for cannabis consumption is not "stoners", but "soccer moms". We tried to be sensitive to their challenges of walking into a retail store. Eventually, the stigmas will begin to fade and in the not-too-distant future, purchasing cannabis will be no more scrutinized than picking up a bottle of wine at the liquor store. Until then, creating an impeccable image and a consistent branding message was and is a top priority.

We have enjoyed robust growth with Strainwise in Colorado and are currently expanding to other states and even Puerto Rico where we are opening up several branded dispensaries. Colorado is reaching the saturation point and while each state has unique challenges, the processes and strategies we learned over the last decade in Colorado help us to provide streamlined, actionable advice to others. In the early stages of our first operation I literally had to be hands on in every aspect of the business. I have potted, trimmed and fertilized plants. I have also been a "budtender" and customer service representative. By default, I've had to be hands on with all aspects of the operations, from inception to finished product sales, which few consultants can claim. I believe it's helped Strainwise to set itself apart from other consulting firms.

With more states coming online for medicinal and recreational cannabis, branding and marketing will become increasingly important. Some believe "cannabis sells itself ", I do not. No different than any other business, smart business practices, effective branding and marketing and social responsibility are essential to initial and long-term success.

In all states, even Colorado, marketing presents a challenge. Traditional vehicles for marketing like radio, newspapers and local to are not viable options for reaching consumers. Currently, retail cannabis stores are relegated to the same alternative papers that are filled with ads for night clubs and strip bars. The industry is growing at an amazing pace and there will be a tipping point when mainstream media can no longer turn away marketing dollars. Even then, what will be allowed in a commercial TV spot?

Commercial breweries and liquor companies spend millions on marketing but even after decades of "accepted marketing", they have restrictions on what they can present. Have you ever noticed that no one ever drinks a beer or cocktail in their TV ads? Advertising restrictions dictate that a glass of wine or mug of beer can be shown, but it cannot be consumed in the ad. We expect a multitude of restrictions to apply to cannabis ads and it will be our duty to adjust and create effective campaigns.

Many business people and entrepreneurs see the obvious, which is almost unprecedented growth in an industry that consumers have been patiently waiting for. The idea that one can open their doors to consumers and make a $10 million dollar profit a year later is absolutely false. Rapid growth breeds competition and there is a LOT of competition. We feel that companies that take the time to ensure they have the right messaging and exceptional products/services will elevate themselves from the pack.

It is my hope, and the hope of all of us at Strainwise, that we can help other companies navigate the regulatory abyss. That we can strategically position them to rise above the fray and not only enjoy the profits but also the goodwill that comes from helping people looking to alleviate pain, lower stress and anxiety or get better sleep. This is what we specialize in.

In hindsight, the collapsed real estate deal that led to our first Strainwise location was a blessing. It forced us to find answers and overcome obstacles. We are proud to have enjoyed the success we've had so far and are proud to share our real-world knowledge with others looking to take part in this amazing industry. If you are in the early stages of business planning or mired in paperwork and legal forms, we can help. To see how we can best support you, we'd love for you to connect with us at Strainwise.

"How can we possible apply logic to business de-cisions when the US government engages in dou-ble-speak? For example, they hold a patent on CBD as a neuroprotectant, and approved Dron-abinol (an exact replica of THC) through the FDA, yet insist cannabis, and its components, have no medicinal benefits. We are taxed more heavily than other industries, but are blocked from having bank accounts to pay our taxes. The obstacles are many, yet we persevere. There are too many lives at stake to walk away. I have witnessed the positive impact cannabis has on patients' health, and it would be unconscionable to stop working to solve the cannabis conundrum."

Mara Gordon, Founder

Aunt Zelda's™, Zelda Therapeutics, The Oil Plant, Calla Spring Wellness

Chapter 5

Changing the Cannabis Conversation via The Hemp Road Trip

Rick Trojan, III

In January 2016, I set out in a biodiesel van to visit 40+ states throughout the United States. Intent on coinciding with the midterm elections, the Hemp Road Trip "bus" set out on a mission aimed at increasing the awareness and understanding of industrial hemp, and ending prohibition. Through a global grassroots campaign, the bus visited 48 states using their opportunity to meet with Presidential candidates, state and federal legislators, along with hundreds of business owners, farmers and interested citizens, passionately working to dispel the misinformation about hemp and sharing the multitude of benefits this amazing plant provides.

Surprised and amazed at the diversity hemp offers, I felt compelled to focus my energy on educating as many people as possible, sometimes whether they wanted to learn or not. Often confused and falsely mistaken as marijuana, the bus and crew encountered both warm welcomes and a fair amount of trepidation and mistrust.

Looking to change things on the political level, and although rarely welcomed with open arms, The Hemp Road Trip Bus visited state capitals, state houses and city halls. While at the state house in Salt Lake City, Utah, the State Police even called in drug sniffing dogs as they prevented entry. Perhaps the biggest conundrum that hemp suffers is the incorrect perception that it is too closely related to marijuana. As the Hemp Bus crisscrossed the US, the team repeatedly educated politicians and their constituents that while it looks very similar, there are many unique differences and benefits to hemp.

Keeping in mind the blend of positive and negative members of my audiences, I was able to impress listeners with the wide-ranging benefits of hemp, which are as significant today, if not more than before. As I traveled through the states, I would often meet and ask consumers if they knew the difference between hemp and marijuana. The answer was all too often, no. With a few examples of some of my favorite hemp facts, even the most skeptical individual found it difficult to not be intrigued. Always with a smile, I made clear to point out and educate everyone I met, that "Hemp is NOT Marijuana". The multitude of commercial uses of hemp, I explained, dates back 12,000+ years and has been used in almost all cultures on nearly every continent throughout known history, including being popular with both the Chinese and Egyptians. The ships that ventured out to discover the New World used hemp to create the sails and ropes. Its high tensile strength and resistance to weather were critically important to our early explorers. Hemp was a widely utilized crop even before the Revolutionary War and some Pilgrims were even required by law to grow hemp. Even George Washington and Thomas Jefferson grew hemp and used hemp paper to draft the Declaration of Independence. In 1937, Popular Mechanics Magazine touted hemp as America's next billion-dollar crop! But somehow, in one of the greatest policy mix ups in US history, hemp has been banned for the last 77 years.

With hemp sales and usage growing at a rate in excess of 25%, you might wonder why I felt the need to go on a National campaign to educate the public and policy makers about hemp.

Americans import over a billion dollars a year worth of hemp products from countries like Canada and China. Since it is a naturally disease and drought resistant crop, hemp is an obvious choice for farmers looking for a sustainable and profitable crop. Besides the more well-known uses like rope and fabric, hemp is a source of Omega-3s, is great as a vegan protein source, can be made into a biodegradable/compostable plastic water bottle, next generation superconductors, and many more uses.

With increased scrutiny on our trade imbalance, my well-timed mission was and still is to have more farmers produce hemp in the US.

Besides spreading awareness across 80% of the US states during the road trip, my associates and I sought out co-sponsors for The Industrial Hemp Farming Act of 2014. It's all part of a movement that is gaining momentum as Americans are seeking to become more environmentally and socially minded by choosing and purchasing organic, renewable and sustainable options. Although hemp is not always 100% organic, it requires far less pesticides than typical crops.

Despite all of the health and commercial benefits derived from hemp, it is still not commercially legal in all 50 states. Congress has made some strides to legalize hemp, but there is a long way to go before it is the widely accepted plant that it was at this nation's inception. As licensing in more states and wider acceptance of hemp happens organically, the costs to produce environmentally sound products like hemp-derived plastics will come down. Currently our oceans are filled with flotillas of plastic, some the size of Rhode Island, littering and impacting marine life and reefs. Informed consumers are increasingly calling for bans on things like plastic straws, plastic water bottles and plastic bags, to name a few. While hemp-based plastics are a green alternative, switching over rapidly to hemp plastics is currently cost-prohibitive.

When used to derive Cannabidiol (CBD), using hemp as a nutritional source or fabric/industrial product, hemp uses far less water and is naturally more resistant to parasite, disease and rot that affect other crops.

Thomas Jefferson once said, "Hemp is abundantly productive and will grow forever on the same spot". It's time that America got back to its roots and valued hemp as much as our great leaders like Jefferson and Washington.

At a recent trade show in Boston, MA, an attendee that listened to me speak, made the analogy that The Hemp Road Trip Bus and Rick Trojan are the modern-day equivalent of John Chapman. Who is John Chapman you ask? He was a farmer in the late 1700s and early 1800s that crisscrossed the US spreading his passion about a particular plant. That plant was the apple tree and you likely know him by his nickname, Johnny Appleseed. With the Hemp Road Trip's campaign mission to enlighten our country about hemp, perhaps decades from now we'll reference these efforts to promote hemp much like we credit the gentleman farmer who had a passion for apples.

With advocates like myself tirelessly informing Americans about the benefits of hemp, and a groundswell of informed consumers looking for more ethical and sustainable products, the tide is definitely changing. Perhaps not as quickly as I and other hemp advocates would like, but there are strides made virtually daily that move the US closer to becoming a significant producer of this time-tested plant. The industry anxiously awaits the final version and passing of the 2018 Farm Bill, which has support on both sides of the aisle for legalization of industrial hemp in the US.

In case you were wondering, I do more than just talk about hemp. You could say I definitely "walk the walk", too. While I take pride in my advocacy efforts, I am also a successful entrepreneur who has achieved "proof of concept" with hemp farming operations in Colorado, Kentucky, North Carolina and Oregon. Being what some would consider a successful entrepreneur, I help found one farming operation that started with 300 acres in 2015 and is now currently one of the single largest growers of hemp in the USA with 1500 acres. In total, my companies are cultivating nearly 2000 acres nationwide.

"I was 10 years old when I sat in the first hearing for Hemp, after the prohibition. Back then, as my mother created the first Hemp garments (the original Ecolution brand), we were mandated to label it as "100% Cannabis Sativa L" in order to legally import into the US. If you are at all familiar with Cannabis, you won't be surprised that this caused every shipment to then be confiscated by Barry McCaffrey himself, the Director of the Office of National Drug Control Policy. This continued until we finally threatened to take him to Supreme Court for harassment. As result, I learned at a very young age to embrace the ignorance that our country had created around Hemp. Coming from a family with 4 generations of natural fiber development and design, the value and opportunities working with Hemp seemed quite natural to me. Our mission has been to educate designers, and people in general, about Hemp and why it is such an important product for their everyday use. We hit the pavement to attend every trade show, industry event, and public forum we could find, and inevitably had to open retail stores to create more outlets for Hemp products. It was imperative to show that a single plant could do so much, outperforming most synthetic materials on the market. While we were confident in its ability, we worked with accredited labs to prove it scientifically. We established enough credible evidence to move hemp forward into many markets we knew would, if not already, be desperate for natural fibers. Over many years of hard work and dedication we have championed Hemp's ability, when grown and processed correctly, to be a sustainable option for the textile and fashion industries. With new blends and weaves, we now have Hemp fabrics that any designer will find a perfect addition to their lines, showing the global community that there are no limits to what hemp fabrics and fashion can do today. We are able to produce a high-quality product while at the same time, protecting our Earth. Sustainability is not a test or a challenge, it is as simple as making the decision and great change can happen overnight. Conscious consumers are proving this every day by supporting healthy products and transparency, and you can't get better when choosing Hemp."

Summer Star Haeske
- Co-Founder,
EnviroTextiles LLC

Chapter 6

U.C.S.: Use Cannabis Safely

David Cunic, PT

Although, I have never been a grower or seller of cannabis, being in the medical field and interacting with Cannabis, I believe I offer a unique position to help shed some light, at least in part, on the "Cannabis Conundrum". I would like to posit several thoughts, observations and concerns along two lines of information concerning Use Cannabis Safely (UCS). The first one is from the medical side, and the other is related to the importance of testing cannabis. Hopefully, this will help to further clear up some of the smoke surrounding the topic, as the subtitle of this book subtly suggests.

My name is David Cunic. Not only am I an accredited licensed Physical Therapist and personal trainer who retains over 15 years of experience in New Jersey, but I am also the original co-founder and chairman of several health and wellness companies. One of my many accomplishments was with a Cannabis focused website that averaged more than one million unique visitors every month. Along with a Bachelor's degree in Health Science, I have earned a Master's degree in Physical Therapy from the University of New England. I also hold numerous certifications in the medical field. With these degrees, I have been honored by speaking at many national conferences, teaching people the principles of UCS: Use Cannabis Safely. My expertise in Orthopedics and Sports Medicine has opened doors for me to work with many sports organizations including professional and Olympic teams, as well as many former professional athletes. My dedication to continuously educate my patients on informed and researched health options, including how to use cannabis safely, has been awarded through my former physical therapy company DMC Athletics & Rehabilitation, Inc. which had been voted #1 in its field many times, including an unprecedented six-year run, from 2006 to 2012, in Morris County, NJ.

The medical cannabis industry is exploding into a very lucrative business. Perhaps you're reading this book as an entrepreneur or investor looking to become more informed before deciding if the business of cannabis suits you. Well, the byproduct of this rapid development comes with both negative and positive side effects. That being said, it is getting harder and harder for people who maintain a negative view of cannabis, to continue to hold onto that outdated and jaded opinion.

On the medical front I would like to make the following statement: Cannabis is a Modern-Day Penicillin. The medical uses of cannabis currently center on two natural chemicals, both of which are derived from cannabis: CBD which is Cannabidiol and THC which is Tetrahydrocannabinol. In a very basic description, CBD is a compound that positively impacts the body is several ways, without the insinuated "high" factor. While THC is very often used for its nausea and pain-relieving properties, with a "high" or euphoric effect to the user. There are hundreds of other natural chemicals found in cannabis that medical experts believe could prove, with further research, to have therapeutic benefits.

The list of medical conditions where cannabis use has a positive effect as a treatment is long and continues to grow rapidly.

This list includes, but is not limited to, some of the following: chronic pain, muscle spasms, seizure disorders such as Dravet syndrome, anxiety, PTSD, dementia, fibromyalgia, cancer, stroke, brain trauma, concussions, glaucoma, Crohn's and IBS, arthritis.

It is my opinion that we should be taking a TRUE medical team approach towards our health care. For example, you might be required to have a basic orthopedic surgery. While the procedure itself may be relatively simple, with preparation for the surgery as well as post-operative, all said and done you might have four or five medical professionals connected as a team that is providing input to that surgery. This medical team might include a primary care physician, a surgeon, a nutritionist, a physical therapist, or a chiropractor. Within this medical team spiderweb, it would only take one medical professional with a negative attitude towards cannabis to ruin that option for treatment as part of your plan of care. It raises the question, "Why would a doctor be against a viable treatment for a patient of theirs?" Excuses used by the medical community may vary. Some doctors may say we don't have enough gold plated double blind studies to prove cannabis as a viable treatment option, so they can't recommend the use. Some medical professionals may say it is not federally legal. Or maybe they just still believe a lot of the negative anti-cannabis propaganda used over the years.

Currently, I have found in my own Physical Therapy business is that there still remains a stigma in the medical community towards the use of cannabis. What I have come to learn from several patients is that many are afraid to ask me about using cannabis as a treatment option and that very often patients hide their use of cannabis from their doctors.

As far as I see it, good information trumps ignorance every time. I know that if doctors are NOT willing to listen and learn about cannabis themselves, it is going to foster a negative doctor-patient relationship among patients who are users of medical cannabis. This negative relationship and fear of the patient being forthright, will push doctor's patients toward other less trustworthy sources for their information. Doctors have a lot of power and influence that they can use to try and help alleviate the seemingly apparent information blackout which continues to be the state of affairs within the medical community.

Doctors need to be able to empower their patients and be willing to listen. There is no push by the medical establishment to educate themselves with the pros and cons of cannabis use. With their medical code of ethics, you would think that a doctor would want to educate themselves about a treatment that has so many positive effects. Now, I will say that there are currently many roadblocks being thrown up by the federal and state governments that inhibit research into the use of cannabis, and specific restrictions to many potentially therapeutic chemicals which can be derived from the same plant. This is why you must cast your eyes abroad towards International research in order to find any current intensive research involving cannabis and its use. From a worldwide perspective, Israel is one of the leading countries where research is currently being conducted.

The tide does seem to be turning bit by bit. I can't say it any better than this quote from the Harvard health blog dated January 15th 2018. Under the title, "Medical Marijuana", Dr. Peter Grinspoon states, "My advice for doctors is that whether you are pro, neutral, or against medical marijuana, patients are embracing it, and although we don't have rigorous studies and 'gold standard' proof of the benefits and risks of medical marijuana, we need to learn about it, be open minded, and above all, be non-judgmental."

More and more people are turning to cannabis as a treatment option for their plan of care. They are learning from a number of sources; friends, celebrities, pro sports players and others. Education is happening and the medical community needs to be a part of that. The shunning and misinformation concerning cannabis use just needs to stop.

The safety of cannabis compared to opioids and other pharmaceuticals seems to be a major factor in the growing acceptance of the plant. Unfortunately, as safe as the plant may be, one of the negative side effects is a result of many people looking to make their claim in the great cannabis gold rush. While a good portion of the community is focused on healing both people and the planet, some of the people who are getting into the growing or selling side of the business are only participating to see how much money they can make from their efforts. Don't get me wrong, I'm all for running a profitable business. In the rush to attain and maximize profits, it's easy to pay little to no attention with regards to product quality or safety. Testing costs money, and not every state has proper testing laws set up to require these cannabis professionals to accurately test their product.

We need to avoid what is happening with the opioid market. These powerful drugs are being overprescribed to the point of detrimental use. Not only are they dangerous and habit forming but they are very costly. Without proper continuing education by the medical community concerning cannabis use we could eventually see the same kind of problems. Better education and information will teach us to avoid many of the problems that we see in the opioid market. You will find cannabis treatment to be more effective and cost less compared to what is out there in the opioid marketplace.

In general, the cannabis industry needs to move past its perceived negative connotations as a whole in order to be fully perceived as a legitimate industry. One way to do this is to require stricter testing standards as you would with any drug. If you are going to be putting anything into your body it would behoove you to make sure it is clean and safe to use. Some states like Nevada and Colorado are already requiring stricter testing standards. The results of this action are somewhat alarming. Colorado has recalled many cannabis products that have been found to contain pesticides and other harmful chemicals that may have detrimental effects on the health of the consumer.

Now I know if you went to the store and bought some oranges you would not be worried about poisoning yourself with pesticides or other harmful chemicals. Why? We know as consumers that the FDA has the proper inspections and testing in place to protect us before the oranges even get to the market. If you were to grow the oranges yourself, you would know if it was grown in a safe, healthy manner. Unfortunately, the ability for most of us to grow our own Cannabis is not an option, therefore it becomes important to research where and how it was grown.

Incorporating testing standards will help to weed out the growers that are careless with how or when they are treating their crops with pesticides or other synthetic chemicals during the growing process. Currently 29 states and Washington D.C. have laws legalizing the use of medical marijuana. Unfortunately, at the same time not all states that allow the use of cannabis have the same kind of strict testing laws as Nevada has. The same rigorous testing standards that our fruit, vegetables, meat and dairy must meet, needs to be implemented in all states planning to or have already legalized cannabis in some form. Consider the recalls we hear about on a regular basis for fruits, vegetables, milk, meat, etc. with standards already in place for some time. Imagine the exposure a newly legal, highly profitable and actively watched industry would suffer if it doesn't welcome and adopt efficient testing. It's not far-fetched to envision the major networks announcing: "cannabis dispensaries and grow facilities throughout the US are destroying thousands of pounds of Brand X from their shelves". As the saying goes, "a few bad apples can spoil the bunch". If comprehensive testing isn't required as part of the emerging industry's standards, it will likely lead to some people offering low quality, potentially harmful products to the market. When people start being harmed from products because of pollutants or other substances such as mold or fecal matter, those looking to cast a shadow over the Cannabis industry will be gifted with talking points that could have easily been prevented by the industry itself. As this industry becomes more of a reality and more of the country has some form of legal cannabis available, testing standards should be required and passed at the same time to promote the safe use of cannabis whether it is being used medicinally or responsibly as an adult.

Just to my North in New England, Massachusetts, Vermont and Maine, all these states have allowed, or are about to allow, recreational cannabis sales, while the remaining New England states of Connecticut and Rhode Island follow close behind. The newly elected New Jersey Governor has supported legalizing adult use cannabis publicly, and the New York

Department of Health just released a report that supports the regulation and legalization of cannabis. If you've lived in or visited the area, you no doubt know that they are all relatively close geographically. Without regulation and continuity of product, you could encounter vast differences in cannabis. The unregulated product will likely be less expensive, so if you live in a state that borders another, the natural tendency would be to get more value through a lower price point.

Not to anyone's surprise, money plays a key role here. As the industry grows, a new revenue stream in the form of taxes and licensing fees gets passed onto the states. In Colorado alone last year (2017), the state took in a whopping $247,368,473 in taxes, licenses and fees (as per www.colorado.gov website). This tax revenue, often bringing in millions of dollars, is making it much easier for states to turn a deaf ear to the proponents against legalization, moving ahead with legislation for the legalization of cannabis.

As more states legalize cannabis, spurred by the new revenue, the ability to tax the industry at a reasonable rate may become an issue. While I don't like to compare the cannabis industry to the toxic cigarette industry, the inherent issues that accompany any increased costs will prove true with cannabis sales. On the border of Connecticut and New York the handful of convenience stores and gas stations do a robust business from cigarette smokers looking to evade the hefty taxes on a pack of smokes and drive to Connecticut to stock up. This happens on the New York and Pennsylvania border as well. The hope is that quality product, at affordable prices, becomes readily available for those looking to consume Cannabis. With that in mind, the new-found revenue from regulating and taxing this industry should go towards repairing and expanding infrastructure, improving community health and education, and other worthwhile programs that promote a better, healthier society.

My goal and takeaways from this chapter: Use Cannabis Safely. Whether you're a doctor or a patient, educate yourself with the pros and cons of cannabis. Tether strict testing requirements along with legalization. Tear down current roadblocks that make further research nearly impossible. You might find that to your delight you will find a treatment option that is more effective and less costly than what you are currently using or considering using.

"Maturing in the world as a Millennial in the 21st century, witnessing paradoxical information and conundrums, that when questioned are only responded to with loquacious regurgitated nonsense, has become something both uneasy to comprehend and accept. The Cannabis conundrum however, in my opinion and experience, is one that tops them all. We must not allow the old seeds of greed, racism, and misinformation against this ever-versatile plant to take root in our world again. Our collective goal should be to break this cycle, embracing the opportunity we have today to solve this conundrum once and for all."

Gerran Bettison-Clark

Imperial Hemp Company, CEO

Chapter 7

I Know I'm Not the Only One

Anonymous Consumer Advocate

My "life" story is a roller coaster of trials and errors, hardships, physical pain from accidents, constant emotional upset and stress. As a child, it started with a lot of physical pain. Since the doctors couldn't locate where the pain stemmed from, I persevered by convincing myself that it was just in my head and that the piercing pains would eventually go away. Depression lent its hand to me at a very young age, as well as anxiety and lack of motivation. Several of my "mental" issues stemmed from negative childhood experiences, including constant teasing by classmates because my skin color was not the same as theirs. It also became apparent that I held a very different view of life in general. I felt abandoned on many levels, however, this taught me at a very young age the significance and value of who to surround yourself with. I was constantly stared at in public establishments and learned, sometimes the hard way, that I was not welcome into some people's homes. But I was a resilient child and eventually mastered the ability to hide my feelings, putting a smile on my face no matter what the circumstance. This eventually led to me struggling with strong inner emotions, always feeling deep down inside that there could be more to this thing we call "life".

As a child, I was eager to learn about life which included love and acceptance. From birth, consumption of knowledge about life is attained from others who you should not be afraid to interact with. Some role models I had to guide me were caretakers, parents, grandparents, siblings, aunts, uncles, friends, teachers, medical professionals, etc. I was taught how to eat, walk, talk, about how I should feel things, including when was the right time to express those feelings. Of course, I was also exposed to both the feelings of love and discrimination. I learned about many types of spiritual and religious beliefs, was taught the difference between what is right and wrong, and so much more. This knowledge set the foundation for how I was to interact within this thing we call "life".

As a typical teen, I had dreams of what my future would hold. It always included the happy life that everyone deserves, the good ole "American Dream". This life would provide prosperity and success for me if I worked hard and embraced all the opportunities that presented throughout my life. This life also would be shared with a husband and possibly kids one day. While I had always strived towards this goal, and to be viewed as an equal in this world, I quickly learned that I actually wasn't. This was a challenging reality to accept.

After a couple years of therapy as a teen, along with several different prescriptions to find the right balance for myself, I was finally "cured". I discovered the miracle of a complete numbing sensation from the pills I was prescribed. My feelings and emotions disappeared to a manageable level and above all, the medications sent the bad thoughts I was having on a daily basis to a campsite in the back of my mind. This lasted a whole two years for me before I had to go back to the doctor as my "cure" started to fail in keeping the "happy" high going for me. The solution? A continuous change of medications and more of them without being able to get back to my "happy" place.

At the age of 18, I finally was able to choose my own path. So, the first thing I decided to do was be truly happy. I stopped all the medications as I convinced myself I didn't need them. I would find a way to manage without them somehow. As expected, major life shifts, good and bad, presented themselves over and over again. Some of these shifts were from gaining successful employment which has guided me to my current career. I moved over 10 times during the course of 20 years due to my ever-changing living situation. At the age of 20, I had my second major life experience with death as I watched a dear friend regress from a healthy 200+ pounds down to 80 pounds in the matter of a couple months. He lost his fight with cancer very quickly. Seeing how it affected his family, which included his 2-year-old daughter, taught me about the precious value of life versus material things. I was introduced to and said goodbye to many families while trying to find my perfect match. This period of time in my life included dating someone with kids, marriage then divorce, having 4 angel babies and of course the blessing of having my own kids. The pinnacle moment came a few short years later when I woke up one day with three young kids, only to be left existing as a single mom, heartbroken... living in physical pain and discomfort every day. I felt an unbearable loneliness which left me with a whole new outlook on what life meant.

Now, the challenge for me was how to survive for my kids, the only concrete part of my heart and in my life. I can't let them down; I have to be "happy" for them to experience happiness. My options? The start of a whole new regimen of pills. I figured I could manage the physical pain with pain medication. That's what it is there for, right? I was prescribed an insomnia medication as I was scared to go to sleep. I thought, "No big deal." I needed my sleep and this helped to keep most of the nightmares away. And let's not forget about that anxiety medication for those constant thoughts and fears of something possibly happening to me. How will my kids end up if I'm not around to help them while they are young? I know these types of questions go through any parent's head, but when it hits home and becomes overwhelming, it becomes all too real.

Fast forwarding a couple years, I crashed hard from it all. I was tired of the doctor game and the plethora of prescriptions. It seemed like everyone was being prescribed the same exact medications. As I attempted to get my prescriptions filled, I had been informed of time and time again from the pharmacies that rules and regulations limit the inventory that can be distributed during the month. That means that there were months that I couldn't even fill my prescription. My biggest concerns though were that most of the pills I was taking long term didn't seem to last as long between doses, and I also started noticing that I was having very negative thoughts and feelings. I now lived in fear, afraid to use up what I was prescribed, worried about running out and experiencing painful withdrawals. I couldn't remember anything. I felt I was going crazy in my own skin. This wasn't happiness. I constantly searched but wasn't able to find a doctor that seemed to care, mainly because I didn't have health insurance. Also, let's not forget to mention that when you're on any type of narcotic, you're automatically labeled the minute you walk through the door even though you beg the doctor to help you get off the medications. Then, while you're walking out of the appointment with the same prescriptions as when you arrived and no plan to get you off of them, it truly leaves you feeling helpless and hopeless. Every time I tried "weaning" myself off everything, it landed me in the hospital from the withdrawals. So, what was I to do but stay on them. For many years I tried to find a solution for my physical pain but as most know, here in the US, the pharmaceutical system is designed to keep customers, not cure them.

I couldn't continue to function, or I should say "not function" like this. I felt that I was letting my kids down, but unsure how I was going to be able to manage the physical and emotional pain without help. After weighing out my options and fear of losing custody of my kids, I decided I would brave it out, in a way where no one would know. I stopped everything cold turkey during the summer months during a time that I didn't have my kids. I wasn't too coherent for the first few days and at some point, I recall continuously passing in and out of consciousness from going without eating or drinking for a few days. I was too physically and emotionally weak to even move. Then, for months after, I experienced constant coldness throughout my body which alternated into hot sweats. I was also weak and fatigued to the point that walking up a single flight of stairs became so exhausting that I would have to stop halfway to rest. After all this, I was left with a very frail and malnourished body that I carefully hid under layers of clothes so that my kids couldn't feel my bones. I tried to seek other pain remedies, including surgery, but in the end, I had to go back onto the same meds I fought so hard to go off. Once again, I felt I had no other options available to me.

Now let's jump to the present... I can positively report that I am completely off all prescribed pills and experienced only minor withdrawals coming off all opioids. I owe this recovery to my decision to use cannabis. One drug to another? I can honestly say that I believe the answer to this question is "NO". It took some time for me to become open to the idea of trying cannabis, mainly because I was always taught it was a drug and bad for you. But after doing some of my own research, which was and is still very limited, I wanted to try it. I had to at least try it, with hopes that I had finally found an alternative option to the pharmaceuticals. I learned it comes in many different forms such as edibles, tinctures, etc. But how would I get it? How did I get it? I would love to tell you all the details, and say it was easy, however I don't feel I can have that voice in today's society yet. When I first began experimenting with cannabis, it wasn't nearly as accepted as it is today. Due to my career choice and the dedication to my kids and all their activities, I was fearful of the consequences I would endure because of the judgment from others if they knew. I had no doubt that my own family would disapprove even though I was suffering daily. Although my concerns were justified, desperate times called for desperate measures. I can personally say that I made the correct choice for myself. The reward was well worth the risk. My life is now "happy" pills free and I can function easier in today's society using cannabis safely and responsibly without the fear of withdrawals or negative effects.

I have agreed to contribute to this book (still anonymously) as it is my hope that the more we talk about, learn about, and research cannabis, that we find ways to help people of all ages, from young children to the elderly. Since using cannabis safely, I have been able to get to meet and know both children and adults who have chosen the same path as myself. I have seen it positively affect so many people where they are able to live a more "normal" life. While the choices I have made are not meant to promote cannabis as a panacea or miracle cure, we are fortunate to be alive during a time where a safer, natural option appears to exist. I only wish I had this option available to me a long time ago. Society is suffering with a multitude of illnesses, both acute and chronic due to mental and physical pain. They turn to what they know, calling on a doctor to help them which commonly ends up in a pharmaceutical prescription. By sharing my personal struggle with the opioid market and other pharmaceuticals, and by being able to find a more effective solution through the safe use of cannabis, I hope more and more people will feel comfortable exploring this medicinal plant as an option for them as well.

My journey and related experiences, while not an easy one, will surely be one with a happy ending. Unfortunately, this may not be the case for everyone dealing with a mental and/or physical illness who already feel they are without a safe alternative or informed place to turn for help. What's needed? More education on cannabis to both doctors and patients/consumers. Our medical system needs to become more personalized and patient centric as no two people are exactly alike, not even identical twins. We need to remove the negative stigmas surrounding cannabis and open our arms to safe, natural, and effective options. A person should no longer have to hide or be ashamed when talking about cannabis, regardless if with your doctor, your employer, your family or friends.

I'll leave you with this: If it was you or your family member suffering, what would you do? I know I hope that one day I can share my knowledge of cannabis with my kids where I won't fear that I will be judged by family and they will be judged by their peers. They are entitled to a safer medicinal alternative to choose from just like everyone else should be.

"Developing a cannabis-infused beverage line, mood33, took many years, multiple false starts and many partners to find our place in the market. Crafting a new category with unique challenges with respect to regulatory compliance and packaging are issues any new consumer brand faces, and it is no different with cannabis products. The harder part is that the industry is segmented into select legal state markets where a brand like mood33 could be launched and sold legally, limiting our ability to grow and reach new audiences. Our original team were all Manhattan or Brooklyn based, making it quite difficult to launch and operate a cannabis brand due to the regulatory limitations and inability to sell cannabis infused food or beverages in New York State. This market condition resulted in me choosing to move myself and my family out to a state where cannabis was fully legal for adults, in the same way many medical cannabis patients have had to move to a new state in order to access their medicine. This sacrifice and risk were necessary for us, but as New York and the rest of the nation start to look at improving their cannabis laws surrounding prohibition - we will look to come 'back home' and share our products and our new found knowledge with the communities we grew up in and built our careers within. Living in a country where all individuals have unobstructed access to legal cannabis is our overarching goal, and by taking the risks to create better-for-you cannabis products and brand experiences should bring that reality into fruition for all much sooner. We dream about the day where folks can find their favorite cannabis products in any state they live in, just as they can with most other health and wellness or medicinal products."

Michael Christopher

Chief Mood Officer & Co-Founder
mood33 Cannabis Infused Sparkling Tonics

Chapter 8

Investing in the Cannabis Industry

Lawrence Schnurmacher

Unless you've been living on a desolate island for the past 5 years, you have no doubt been touched in some way by the explosive growth of the cannabis industry. Pretty much every day of the week brings news about states that are moving to legalize cannabis either medicinally or for recreational/adult use. With unprecedented growth comes opportunity. Opportunity to experience the myriad health and lifestyle enhancements associated with this plant and the opportunity to benefit financially by investing in the companies that will be critical to this growth.

The conundrum is how and where does one invest? Although the tide is slowly changing, many financial vehicles don't or won't offer any cannabis-related businesses to their clients. Investors have had some flexibility to choose categories like green/environmentally responsible companies, socially responsible companies, high risk, low risk, etc. Even amongst 401 k's there are often numerous options, but not so with cannabis-related companies. However, in countries like Canada, we see large sums of investment capital flowing into cannabis related companies. While it is not easy to invest in companies that are part of the booming cannabis wave, it is getting easier. The real conundrum is what types of companies to invest in.

My name is Larry Schnurmacher and I am the managing partner at Phyto Partners. We are a venture capital firm that seeks out companies that are well positioned to benefit as the wave of legal cannabis spreads throughout the US. You may be surprised to learn that to date, we have not invested in a single grower or retailer of cannabis. As the price of cannabis fluctuates and availability increases, the companies we invest in for our clients are not impacted.

Why don't we invest in growers and retailers? What else is there? There is an old truism that says: "The only people that really made money during the gold rush were those selling the picks, shovels and pans." Historically this is mostly true. Similarly, we are targeting the "picks & shovels" used in the life cycle of cannabis.

To understand our philosophy at Phyto Partners, let me explain where we see the industry going and why we look for companies outside the obvious grow/retail side of the business. As of the printing of this book, there are in excess of 9 states that already have legal recreational use and 30 states with legal medicinal use. It took decades for the first states to put legalization on the ballot. With early adopters like Colorado and Washington showing not only that cannabis legalization can happen relatively seamlessly, but also drive hundreds of millions in taxable revenue, surrounding states began to take notice.

Many have made the analogy of the growth of the cannabis industry to that of the Dot.com boom or growth of the internet. Another comparison is far more accurate in my eyes - Prohibition. Like alcohol during prohibition years, consumers have discreetly purchased cannabis, albeit illegally, for decades. As legalization increases, so will the acceptance and use. We expect in the not too distant future to be able to sit down for a nice dinner and choose a THC infused dessert perhaps. Or, in addition to grabbing a six pack and bottle of wine at the grocery store, picking up pot brownies or perhaps a yogurt with a strain of cannabis that helps with sleep.

In short, we expect cannabis to be widely available in a multitude of products. So, tell me again why we don't advocate investment in the growing and selling of cannabis? Make no mistake, there will be growth and profits for those focused on those elements. The "hidden growth" we see comes from the companies we identify as being critical to the distribution, processing, tracking, testing, etc.

Let me give you an example. We recently invested in a temp staffing firm that specializes in workers who are licensed or certified to work with cannabis grow operations. Although states are allowing the growth and sale for consumption, they are unanimously stringent about who is allowed to own, grow and sell cannabis. During the harvest at a large grow operation, the mature buds on acres of cannabis can require harvesting within a short window. Unlike other produce, growers of cannabis can't simply hire scores of migrant workers, they need licensed and vetted personnel.

The same goes for a retail store that has a few workers call in sick or quit. They need to be replaced by licensed, screened & vetted employees. While large temp firms like ADT don't offer this service (yet), we invested in a company that is well positioned to be the leader in cannabis staffing needs. These are the picks and shovels of the cannabis industry.

Our strategy is to comb through the thousands of companies hanging a shingle out and jumping into this rapid growth industry and identify those with solid leadership and a must-have service or product. Regardless of what an ounce of cannabis goes for, companies like the aforementioned staffing service will thrive.

Perhaps the greatest advantage we have, is that this industry is truly in the infancy stage and identifying the companies that are key to the overall success early will be financially rewarding. There are so many crucial elements throughout the supply chain: testing and standardization, payment processing, transportation, security, marketing, etc.

In the not too distant future, we expect that besides seeing Budweiser and Coors commercials during the Super Bowl half time show, you'll see cannabis products. What agencies will produce those spots? Agencies that we would consider investing in. You get the point.

Some might suggest that the exploding cannabis market is the tide that floats all boats, that you can't go wrong by investing in any of the companies that are part of this truly historical market growth. Who wants any company? We look for exceptional companies that add value to the infrastructure of the cannabis industry and in turn provide our clients with exceptional gains; companies that we can invest in and realize a profitable exit strategy.

At Phyto Partners, our job is to evaluate and weed through the thousands of companies taking part in this revolution and offer only those that are low risk but have a huge potential up-side. I welcome a call to go more in detail about our portfolio of companies. These are exciting times and for those investing, we would love the opportunity to help you benefit financially.

Chapter 9

Corporate Social Responsibility in the Cannabis Industry

Heidi Parikh

There are a growing number of cannabis nonprofit organizations across the world, many demonstrating that fundraising in the cannabis industry is possible, mainly through grassroots campaigning, (pun intended). The environment for fundraising in the cannabis industry isn't easy though. Challenges include issues of advocating for a schedule 1 substance which many lives and families have been shattered from. The culture of cannabis prohibition has been going on for so long, I wouldn't be surprised it isn't affecting our genetic structure.

On the other side of the fence, we have the biggest industry in the world since the invention of the automobile, exploding with canna-businesses. Every entrepreneur is looking how to make it and making it in this industry usually cost money, lots of it! The competition is fierce and unfortunately even 501(c)(3) nonprofit organizations are looked at as either competition or criminals, making it next to impossible to attract donors.

Credibility is a Necessary Currency

As I said above, one of the biggest challenges these cannabis nonprofits face is the constant struggle to be taken credible. Unfortunately, there happens to be good reason for this. Most people do not understand the vast difference between a state nonprofit and a 501(c)(3) federal nonprofit. Most all dispensaries were advised to open as a state nonprofit rather than a for-profit corporation because most state laws do not allow for an individual to profit.

In a state nonprofit, there is no accountability to the public of what is occurring in the inner workings of a state nonprofit organization, and the owners can take all the money.

Compared to a federal nonprofit, books are requested to be open always, and publishing yearly annual statements occur on Guidestar.Gov. The founders traditionally volunteer thousands of hours to the mission and do not take any of the funds raised if they leave the organization. Many cannabis nonprofits are run as state nonprofits, with no requirement to abide by ethical public policy with regard to transparency, which is a key difference compared to the path through federal nonprofit policy. With no effective regulation of the rapidly expanding cannabis sector in the U.S., opportunities for corruption are rife. Standards of transparency and accountability are poor, with few cannabis nonprofits disclosing information on funds received or how they were used. The media regularly carries stories of charity scams in other parts of the nonprofit sector but has yet to show the skeletons of cannabis nonprofits, maybe because there's only a handful. Despite the public skepticism, cannabis nonprofit organizations, like My Compassion, with solid reputations based on real track records, are still generating support.

Another related concern when addressing credibility is the unfortunate, and all too common, predatory behavior which occurs when a person or loved one is faced with an illness. People will take extreme and drastic measures to help someone in need. While this is an amazing representation of humanity and the power of community, there are those who look to take advantage of that same compassion and generosity. Donations made to organizations are meant to go towards a cause, or to help a group of individuals or families in need. People buying cannabis products through a state nonprofit organization are normally looking to heal or at minimum reduce discomfort, but many times they walk away with a low-quality product from a salesperson posing behind a nonprofit to personally gain.

Of course, this can and does happen in most industries, but as cannabis trends continue to garner attention, and industry to consumer education lags, a cultural shift will demand more from everyone, including both for profit and nonprofit organizations.

Raising Awareness…and Capital

If you think of the overall cannabis market as a continuum with cannabis charities on one end and cannabis businesses on the other, the social cannabis marketplace, then is in between. It most certainly includes social cannabis businesses, businesses that not only make a profit, but also contribute some sort of social impact (like green energy solutions or simplistic horticultural systems). And there are emerging cannabis investment vehicles that can provide investors a financial return (many times over the traditional market rate return) in addition to a social cannabis impact return. But the social cannabis market must also include new financial vehicles for cannabis nonprofit organizations.

Social impact is not a new thing. Many of the financial vehicles being created in the emerging cannabis space are exciting and new whilst creating social impact through entrepreneurial efforts. To effectively provide the public goods that for-profit businesses (both cannabis and social cannabis businesses) can't or won't provide, cannabis nonprofit organizations are essential. Cannabis nonprofit organizations are very much part of this conversation in this emerging market, but still require seed funding, growth capital, capacity capital, loans, equity, grants, operating revenue and so on. Cannabis nonprofit fundraisers can face serious, practical challenges in simply operating.

While gaining acceptance, the banking system may likely not facilitate regular "giving" due to the possible sources of the donations coming or going to cannabis-related business or activities, raising concern about money laundering charges. Writing a check could come under the radar of FINCEN - Financial Criminal Enforcement Network, utilized by the banking system to track and shut down bank accounts that look like money laundering schemes. As with culture and banking systems, the degree to which governments tax nonprofits, or offer any form of tax incentives to donors, varies enormously. This is even more so the case in the cannabis industry, when many aspects of cannabis cultivation, dispensing, testing and processing, can't be written off due to IRS issues.

Something as simple as using the U.S. Postal System to send collateral to prospective donors can get complicated, as the postal system might not be friendly to displaying cannabis images.

There are creative ways around most of these problems but following the laws and requirements of the IRS guidelines is what has allowed a few cannabis nonprofit organizations, like My Compassion, to operate for 10 years in the Medical

Cannabis Industry. Their reason for "being" has always been to create a vehicle for public cannabis education, one that addressed important topics and helps individuals who are not being supported by the general cannabis market. While the effort is sincere, this isn't to say that it has all been easy. The cannabis industry is still in an early, transformative stage, and strong organizations will adapt and adjust…or disappear.

Improvement Through Innovation

Let's not get bogged down in polarizing opinions and factions, but rather let's take a bigger picture view of the essence of what we are attempting to do: to completely reconfigure and create a productive convergence among the three sectors in the cannabis marketplace.

Most of us would agree that for far too many decades, the government sector's relationship to the cannabis sector has been pretty much broken. Many would also agree that the nonprofit sector, and the philanthropy that funds it, are also highly dysfunctional. Instead of only focusing on making it, we must work together towards a solution, without discounting or dismissing either sector. In the true spirit of the social innovation space, we must recycle and reuse the cannabis nonprofit and government sectors, just as we are refashioning the private cannabis sector. We must reconfigure the assets of all three sectors to turn them into more effective, more productive, higher functioning sectors that can work with, not separate from, each other to create collaborative solutions.

So, what might that look like?

It means that:

- Venture philanthropy funds are sharing cannabis investor prospects with social venture funds and vice versa.

- Investors interested in a social return have portfolios that include not only social businesses, but also cannabis nonprofit deals.

- Foundations are investing in both for profit and nonprofit social impact cannabis organizations.

- Identifying that charitable nonprofits like My Compassion are the liaison to the public for businesses and government and help increase consumers in the industry especially one plagued with fear and misinformation.

- Most cannabis nonprofit organizations that have an interest in and capacity for growth have access to growth capital and management expertise to scale.

- A nonprofit that is solving social problems surrounding cannabis is just as sexy and gets just as many resources, respect and mind-share as a cannabis business that is doing the same.

- Those working on changing laws to help cannabis entrepreneurs look at both for profit and nonprofit structures, incentives and restrictions.

The creation of the social cannabis market is a bold, chaotic, possibly insane, but potentially game-changing endeavor that has the power to completely rework how money flows through the market and shape society. Now that would be innovative.

People over Profits

Regardless of sector, size, industry or countless other factors, cannabis business leaders throughout the U.S. face similar challenges: how to boost business, recruit and retain top talent and demonstrate a commitment to community investment. For many companies, continuing to be seen as a business and community leader increasingly requires an effective corporate social responsibility (CSR) program that not only engages staff in local communities but also connects employees to company and business objectives, and demonstrates to the public a tangible commitment to positive corporate citizenship. Research shows just how valuable that social responsibility is for businesses:

- 90 percent of American consumers are more likely to trust and be more loyal to cause-oriented companies (Reference: Cone Communication),

- 80+ percent of consumers consider CSR when deciding what products to buy or recommend to others, which companies they want to see in business in their community and where they would like to work, (Reference: Cone Communication)

- Young professionals who regularly participate in workplace volunteer activities are nearly twice as likely to be satisfied with the progression of their career than those employees who are not engaged in such activities (Reference: Deloitte Volunteer IMPACT survey),

- Companies with integrated corporate citizenship programs saw a significant increase in employee retention
  – a critical benefit considering the financial implications
  of replacing, versus retaining, employees (Reference:
  Center for Corporate Citizenship)

As a nonprofit executive, I've seen firsthand the caring power
of a few in the cannabis community, and I recognize it's not a
small endeavor for companies to balance limited resources,
multiple worthy asks for financial and human resource support
and the need to quantify a valuable return on investment.
While no approach to corporate citizenship is a one-size-fits-
all solution, keeping the following in mind when developing a
CSR strategy can help maximize and amplify your charitable
efforts in the emerging cannabis industry.

Focus giving to a cause that aligns with your company's goals.
When you contribute to a good cause in your community that
directly impacts the success of your business, it's a win-win
situation for everyone involved. By focusing support for organizations that reflect your company's values and mission, you
bring your company to life in a way that you can never imagine, while at the same time strengthening your bottom line. A
word of advice; do not try and do your own community outreach, unless that is what you do for a living. Educating the
masses is time-consuming, and time is money! Focus on your
business development and make tax deductible donations to a
501(c)(3) nonprofit organization that has a track record for doing it well!

Engaging customers has never been more important than in
this industry. With the shift in how consumers view corporate
responsibly, they prefer to spend their money with companies

that support important social causes, and this is one of the biggest in our life time! Engaging customers as a strategy has never been more advantageous to business development than in the medical cannabis marketplace. Consumers believe that companies should not only work to achieve their business goals but do so while also contributing to improving their community. Many people even today see any form of cannabis as a detriment to their community. It is that mentality that makes 501(c)(3) nonprofit organizations so important. Their outreach programs are designed to give not take, the only motive is providing education and that's what is needed to attract loyal customers who will continue to support and expand this market, both medical and recreational.

Empower employees! It's not just consumers who look to associate with socially minded cannabis organizations – employee attraction and retention rates are directly related to social responsibility. Research by CR Strategies found that when employees perceive their employers as socially responsible, they have more positive attitudes in performance-related areas, like customer service. Involving employees in your CSR goals is an essential element of a successful program. By connecting your CSR strategy to your staff's goals, passions and values, you can improve performance, retain top performers, better engage team members with organizational priorities and foster a sense of community among colleagues.

Participating in nonprofit programs collaboration plays an important role in making a difference, and being embedded into a nonprofit's programs help ensure you're making the greatest impact possible. Programs like My Compassion Cannabis Patient Relief (CPR) Program, bolster the collective impact of employee volunteer engagement by boosting collaboration between the business and nonprofit, resulting in a broader, amplified reach. Working together boosts and improves impact: the more voices and ideas that are at the table, the greater impact on the community each program member can have from business stakeholders to receiving program participants and everyone in between. Corporate citizenship is a powerful tool and a win-win for businesses, nonprofits and the community at large. When it's made a priority, it has tangible effects on talent development, business objectives and employee morale – and that translates into thriving businesses and better communities.

Investing in and supporting causes and cannabis nonprofits that strengthen our community doesn't just make good business sense – it turns our region into a place where people want to live, work and raise their families. For more tips on building a cannabis CSR strategy and making the most of your community engagement, visit My Compassion at www.mycompassion.org.

"The reverence one realizes while being witness to the birth of an anomalous industry, is surpassed only by the opportunity to contribute in its re-markable revolution. Whether an individual or organization chooses to contribute or simply exploit the opportunities presently available, will dictate the success of the industry as a whole."

Andrew Young

Project Coordinator at Harvest Inc.

Chapter 10

Can Cannabis Be Sustainable?

D. Jacob Mitchell

The short answer is yes, but let me set the scene first. Almost everything can be sustainable. Every goal that we humans undertake on a daily and generational basis can be made sustainable. Every endeavor we have ever tackled as a species can be done in a way that allows us to live in tandem with our environment instead of constantly trying to crawl over it and beat it like some bully playing king of the hill. Here's the truth, we're never going to win that game.

That's the thing about our relationship to the environment, too many think we are separate from it, above it all. The reality from that is so far from the truth, in fact it is very much the opposite. We depend on Nature. We owe everything to it. When I say everything I mean everything, literally everything you have ever had or will ever own has been made possible by the natural world around us. When you look at the problem this way it suddenly becomes much clearer that sustainability isn't just a good idea for the sake of protecting some trees and animals, it is a necessity for human survival. If you don't fight for Nature for Nature's sake, fight for Nature for humanity's sake. Nature will continue to progress whether we are here or not.

Now, we are unfortunately on the defensive. We are beginning to realize as a society the importance of protecting Nature, but we've already created all these modern industries that were built without it in mind. We're backpedaling in an attempt to retrofit these industries and reduce, mitigate, and otherwise innovate to make them sustainable enough to last. That is why cannabis and sustainability are the perfect blend (besides all the hippies). We have the opportunity to create an entirely new industry sector and do it sustainably. Not in 30 years when it is too late, after we've assessed all the damage, but rather now, before any of it even happens.

Solutions (Larger Picture)

Let's look at the big picture and give ourselves a broader outlook on the main components of this new business environment. There are three major players in this arena. In the first corner, we have "The Regulatory Body". In the other corner, we have companies and industry leaders or "The Producers". The last player, is the whole crowd watching this cage match; they are "The Consumers". These groups all rely on one another to function. Collectively, they create the landscape for the cannabis industry and how it relates to sustainability.

The Regulatory Body is whichever group has deemed it legal for cannabis to be sold recreationally or medically and therefore gets to decide which laws and regulations govern the industry. Currently, this is on a state-by-state basis but eventually it will be in some way handled at a national level. Perhaps even enforced by the ATF. Regulatory Bodies have the power to create rules and regulations which enforce or incentivize sustainable business operations. They are heavily influenced by both consumers and producers in order to get the right balance in their governance.

The Producers are any company that is related to the cannabis industry. This includes dispensaries, concentrate labs, edible kitchens, grow operations, lighting companies, packaging producers, soil companies, nutrient companies, and every other auxiliary company you can imagine. These folks have the power to create a product that their consumers enjoy while shifting the landscape to one more environmentally friendly. This in turn effectively contributes to their story and marketing, increases their revenue, and ensures a viable long-term plan for improvement. They are heavily influenced by their consumers and the market as well as regulatory bodies.

Finally, we have The Consumers. Now this group is by far the largest and potentially the most powerful. Although, we may all be individuals making up this group, we are the base that the producers and the regulatory bodies stand on. We have the ability to influence both other parties by voting with our dollar and, well, literally voting. Look at what happened with Walmart, they stopped carrying milk with antibiotics in it, not for any moral reason but because people stopped buying it. The consumers can create a demand for sustainable cannabis products and the producers will be forced to supply.

Now, we have to understand the people in these groups and their motivations. Intrinsic Sustainability refers to those who undertake sustainability because they believe in it and have such strong values for the environment it overrides traditional business acumen; basically, just doing it because it is right. Others have seen the business case for sustainability; that using less resources, creating efficiency, reducing waste, generating their own energy, saving on fuel costs, (need I go on), is good for their bottom line and the long-term operations of their business. Point being, it doesn't matter which angle you are approaching sustainability from because it benefits everyone.

It is only by combining the strength of these three groups and continuously demonstrating the effectiveness of sustainability in a manner that engages differing viewpoints, will we be able to create a sustainable cannabis industry. We all need to be working together in order to form a future we can all be proud of, pulling in experts from every industry. We need to collaborate to create research on the industry and its impact, as it is severely lacking. We must be adaptable and resilient to a changing future and a budding industry. We have to keep up as the market shifts and continuously improve our processes, we can't go backwards as we get bigger. We have to put together concrete plans for businesses and regulatory agencies with practical results and a feasible return on investment. We have to produce good healthy cannabis grown naturally.

The Issues and Solutions (case-by-case basis)

Before we go deeper into addressing the cannabis sustainability issue, and in order to establish a baseline of knowledge, we need to dive a bit into "what is sustainability"? Sustainability in its most literal sense means to "continue a defined behavior indefinitely". Now, in our case, the defined behavior is "existing" and this we can break down even further into three main parts: People, Planet, and Profit. Known for the most part as the Three P's. Sustainability needs to be holistic in order for it to work. Each pillar must be equally as strong as the pillar next to it. Any problem that falls under one of these categories heavily impacts the other two.

We can use this framework for looking at the reasoning and impact behind making sustainably driven solutions. As the cannabis industry matures and becomes increasingly ambitious, using practical and feasible sustainability solutions to lower business costs and increase efficiency can make organizations more resilient and competitive. Increasing employee benefit programs and community engagement not only emboldens a company's story but will help the entire cannabis industry be seen in a more wholesome light. Protecting the environment will not only produce a cleaner and more holistic cannabis, but it will also ensure the lasting resources needed for the industry to continue into the future. These categories affect each other constantly, and undertaking any development in either category will send ripples into the other two. In order to start pushing down these three roads simultaneously, we have to first understand the problems facing the industry.

Growing Methods

As with any agricultural product, the quality of the plant is dependent on the quality of care you put into it. Personally, I prefer my cannabis grown in a way that is natural and clean of any sort of dangerous toxins, especially if I'm inhaling it.

While the industry has lived so long in the shadows, growers were willing to use any method to produce their cannabis, as long as it gave them a leg up. Obviously, this isn't true of every grower, but unless there is change, this could certainly lead to problems with larger scale, commercial applications. Cannabis will certainly move in the direction of a commercial agriculture product, and unless kept a close eye on, as the industry expands this could lead to less than sustainable cultivation practices. We have seen some of these problems within the food industry already. Thankfully, some of the more popular but unhealthy pesticides and fertilizers, such as Eagle 20, have already been banned.

A healthy plant starts with a healthy soil. By using methods such as "living" soils and polycultures, a nutrient-rich environment can be created without the use of artificial fertilizers. Processes like Integrative Pest Management in which predatory bugs are added to the crop in order to stave off harmful insects negate the need for pesticides. Natural methods also result in a potent cannabinoid/terpene profile and cleaner smoke. As for the industrial agriculture problem, it is up to the consumer to demand a clean product and support small mom and pop grows in the same way micro-brews invaded the beer scene.

Energy

Cannabis cultivation is a very energy-intensive practice, especially when grown indoors. Indoor currently is not the most common type on the market today at only around 18% according to High Times magazine, but accounts for an almost equal percentage of the impact. It is estimated that in 2012, 1% of total electricity usage in the United States and 3% of usage in California in that year went to recreational cannabis cultivation[1]. To be fair, the study this number is cited from has had some holes poked in it over the years but that's about 2 million US homes worth of energy, 7 large power plants worth. In 2014, Denver's cannabis industry used 1% of total electricity

---

[1] Mills, E. (2012). The carbon footprint of indoor Cannabis production. *Energy Policy*. doi:10.1016/j.enpol.2012.03.023

produced for the city and in 2018 that number is at 4%[2], that's a 400% increase in 4 years. Over half of this energy is going to HVAC and dehumidification systems, the next biggest drain being lighting at 38% average consumption for indoor cultivation operations.[3] It takes around 1,200 kHz to grow a pound of cannabis, more than an average US household uses in a month.[4]

Luckily, these numbers are starting to go down as producers see the benefit of creating more efficient lighting systems due to the massive reduction of their energy costs, which can be up to 50% of their total operating costs.[5] The best solution for the energy usage in the industry is to simply grow Cannabis the way it was supposed to be grown: outdoors. In its natural environment, you don't need the expensive air circulation sys-

---

[2] Hood, G. (2018, February 14). Nearly 4 Percent Of Denver's Electricity Is Now Devoted To Marijuana. Retrieved from http://www.cpr.org/news/story/nearly-4-percent-of-denver-s-electricity-is-now-devoted-to-marijuana

[3] Northwest Power and Conservation Council Memorandum - Electrical Load Impacts of Indoor Commercial Cannabis Production

[4] Kolwey, N. (2017, December). A Budding Opportunity: Energy Efficiency Best {Practices For Cannabis Grow Operations. Retrieved from https://www.swenergy.org/data/sites/1/media/documents/publications/documents/A Budding Opportunity Energy efficiency best practices for cannabis grow operations.pdf

[5] Kolwey, N. (2017, December). A Budding Opportunity: Energy Efficiency Best {Practices For Cannabis Grow Operations. Retrieved from https://www.swenergy.org/data/sites/1/media/documents/publications/documents/A Budding Opportunity Energy efficiency best practices for cannabis grow operations.pdf

tem and multitudes of light, the earth does it all for you for free. Obviously, this is not an option for everyone (especially those in metropolitan areas), but as cannabis legalization sweeps the nation, we will see less production in states with poor growing climates and a push to outdoor cultivation, in that way the problem might partially solve itself. For the time being, we can focus on pushing towards greenhouse operations, on-site renewable energy production, and making indoor operations as energy efficient as possible by utilizing LED systems and more efficient HVAC equipment with a strong focus on the insulation properties of the grow.

Water

Every plant needs water in order to grow and keep itself upright. Each pound of flower produced uses a total of 100-150 gallons of water,[6] or 100 toilet flushes. Compare that to corn and it is pretty similar, at about 147 gallons of water per pound. As the industry grows, its overall water usage will as well, and the efficiency may even get worse as large-scale agricultural practices are undertaken. This problem gets even more compounded in states with water issues such as California, where drought is prevalent.

Wastewater is also a large issue as most water from grow operations have a multitude of fertilizers and nutrients in them that are not healthy for the environment (at least in the concentration they are finding). By implementing efficiency options such as drip irrigation and then tackling both these is-

---

6 Writer, M. S. (2015, September 22). Report on Water Usage. Retrieved from https://www.marijuanaventure.com/report-on-water-usage/

sues simultaneously through wastewater recycling, we can not only reduce the amount of total water used, but we can also stop any pollution from causing even greater environmental problems.

Waste

Waste in the Cannabis industry comes from many diverse sources, depending on what aspect of its production you are focusing on. In three and a half years the state of Washington produced 1.7 million pounds of cannabis plant waste, about the same amount that both Colgate and the Philadelphia Eagles produce annually interestingly enough. That is just plant waste though, that doesn't take into account soil waste, packaging waste, operational waste, office waste, cartridge waste, and other edible or consumable product related waste. Now, couple that with the other legal states waste, with more geared up to go legal soon, and you have an enormous amount of waste being generated from this industry that is primarily going to landfills.

Cannabis is a natural material with hosts of imaginative possibilities for waste diversion like composting and reusing the plants nutrients in the next batch or even as animal feed! Grows can use a method for their soil that keeps it healthy and rich, thus eliminating the need for throwing away each batch while saving money at the same time. Dispensaries can incentivize better packaging and "bring back" programs with discounts or deposits. If customers and dispensaries demand a better option, then companies who produce the packaging will need to research and develop more sustainable options. If done correctly, the waste from this industry could be used in a responsible and beneficial way.

Regulations: Friend or Foe?

Speaking of waste, let's use it as an example of how regulations can go awry even with the best of intentions. Cannabis products in Colorado have to leave the store with very specific labeling of their ingredients and disclaimers in a child-proof container (both of which I agree with). This has created an environment where the cheapest option wins and more aesthetic looks requires multiple layers of packaging. Containers can only be reused in the store if the customer washes it thoroughly before bringing it back in the store. It can also only be brought back to the store at which it originated because each store labeling is different. You see how convoluted this gets. Most packaging can be recycled but in the early stages of the legalization there were arguments against it as it was undocumented transfer of cannabis. Also, in Colorado, Cannabis waste from grows must be disposed of in a manner that makes it unusable for human consumption, unless you are zoned for agriculture. Most dispensaries with grows, unless they are far from the cities, are zoned industrial. Methods of disposal I've seen include mixing it with paper shreds and isopropyl alcohol or a lawnmower and store brand Windex.

It is crucial that more conscious regulations are put in place which allow for sustainable disposal and encourage other sustainable options being integrated into the industry. Regulations can be used in a way that ensures responsible business practices while actively mitigating environmental degradation. There is a way to not only discourage poor behavior, but encourage good behavior. For example, incentive programs offering rebates for efficiency upgrades would be fairly easy to implement, and could be used by the company towards marketing and PR too.

In order to enjoy legal cannabis, the industry has had to adjust and manage all types of regulations and requirements necessary to be in business. I'm sure they will put up with ones that ensure a well-treated environment, too.

Carbon

Climate change is one of the most serious issues the world faces today and every industry contributes to it including cannabis. According to an analysis conducted by Evan Mills for each kilogram of cannabis produced, roughly 4,600 kg of CO_2 is emitted. Now, this number is highly disputed and should be reassessed, but that is roughly the equivalent of driving a car for seven and a half days non-stop. Other associated emissions such as delivery of product, consumer driving to store, and disposal of packaging are important to include as well as any production processes, such as edibles or concentrates. Many concentrate producers use massive ventilation systems to pump out the excess butane and propane into the surrounding area, which are both greenhouse gases and contribute to the climate change capacity of the industry.

Companies need to be assessing their impact and mitigating it as much as possible in order to create a longer lasting opportunity for the industry. Completing a carbon footprint assessment gives the business an advantage, providing a tool to see their resource usage and gaps where they may be able to input sustainable measures. Cannabis is an agricultural product, and as such will be very heavily influenced by a changing climate. In fact, cannabis is in a very interesting position where if done correctly, it could have a massively low carbon footprint due to its own carbon sequestration. The plant actually pulls carbon out of the atmosphere and uses it to grow before returning it to the soil. If cannabis is to be feasible for decades than we need to recognize the problem and do our part; only with everybody working towards this issue will we be able to overcome it.

It is important to understand that the categories outlined above will shift and change as the industry does, requiring successful companies to stay adaptive in order to stay on top of the industry. As cannabis legalization expands globally, the issues will change and need to be addressed in the context of the specific needs of that region. In order for the industry to become sustainable as a whole, it will take a greater effort on behalf of all involved and society to be in support of the effort.

These are only general examples of solutions to some issues we see today. Sustainability is an iterative process and therefore must be focused on finding the best possible options for each individual organization or location. There isn't a blanket solution for this which is why cannabis companies need to be working with sustainability experts in order to get the right fit for them. A professional cannot only make you sustainable in a holistic way but they can help you be prepared for a changing industry. A sustainable business is adaptable and resilient.

Summary

In summation, sustainability in the cannabis industry is more than just projects and good planning, it is proving that we are a legitimate industry and we are here to undertake it responsibly. We are at the very beginning, and have the opportunity to set ourselves apart as an industry that operates for change, something we did when we first legalized it. Let's continue setting ourselves apart and in that way, make cannabis the leader and the pioneer for new industries everywhere.

RESOLUTION

As this book winds down towards an end, a final conundrum becomes blatantly apparent. Although the preceding pages offer insightful commentary, opinions and information from a credible group of industry experts, insiders and influencers, we have only just scraped the surface as it relates to the conundrums surrounding Cannabis.

There are many more voices, experiences and perspectives which deserve the opportunity to be shared. With this in mind, it is my resolution and commitment to help continue the conversation, organizing and publishing additional volumes of The Cannabis Conundrum. This is just the beginning…

Future editions will look to include chapters from medical professionals, patients, Cannabis researchers, and many others. We will also take a look at Cannabis from the International perspective, as we realize the world has become much smaller and the legalization of Cannabis is a global issue.

Thank you for taking the time to learn more about Cannabis and the Cannabis Industry.

Please visit **www.TheCannabisConundrum.com** for more info on our contributors, book signings in your area, special events, and more!

Wishing you all the best in health & happiness,

Made in the USA
Columbia, SC
10 October 2018